D0912955

Crosscurrents/MODERN CRITIQUES

Crosscurrents/MODERN CRITIQUES

Harry T. Moore, *General Editor*

Jules Laforgue
ESSAYS
ON A POET'S LIFE
AND WORK

EDITED BY *Warren Ramsey*

WITH A PREFACE BY
Harry T. Moore

SOUTHERN ILLINOIS UNIVERSITY PRESS
Carbondale and Edwardsville

FEFFER & SIMONS, INC.
London and Amsterdam

841.8
L167xN

Copyright © 1969 by Southern Illinois University Press
All rights reserved
"Laforgue in America: A Testimony," first published in The Sewanee
Review, is copyright ©1963 by Malcolm Cowley
Library of Congress Catalog Number 69–11503
Printed in the United States of America
Designed by Andor Braun

Preface

This many-sided exploration of Jules Laforgue is a noteworthy contribution to our understanding of modern poetry, which the too-often-neglected Laforgue helped to develop. The book is timely, for our expanding knowledge and criticism have reached a point at which Laforgue can at last be truly appreciated.

For many Americans their first acquaintance with Laforgue was in the pages of Edmund Wilson's Axel's Castle in 1931. Wilson gave a fairly full picture of Laforgue's career and showed how parts of his poem "Légende" were closely akin to T. S. Eliot's "The Love Song of J. Alfred Prufrock."

Yet other Americans had known of Laforgue, as Malcolm Cowley shows in his essay in the present volume. As a young poet in the 1920's, Cowley openly acknowledged the influence of Laforgue. In Cowley's present essay, and elsewhere in this book, Ezra Pound's missionary work in the recognition of Laforgue is discussed: in 1918, Pound dealt importantly with Laforgue in an issue of the Little Review.

Officially, Laforgue had at least been noticed in standard literary histories. There is for example A History of French Literature, by C. H. Conrad Wright of Harvard, published in 1912 by the Oxford University Press. In its 964 pages, however, the book makes only two slight references to Laforgue, one of them in a footnote which speaks of Laforgue and Gustave Kahn as the two poets who should be "rightly considered" as the initiators of verse libre. The other reference is also in a footnote: "Among the minor Symbolists were Jules Laforgue (1860–1887), whose matter and manner may be summed up in his line: 'Ah! que

la vie est quotidienne!' or his laments on the 'eternullité' of the world." Wright's book is not particularly
stodgy, and in giving Laforgue such hasty treatment he
was perhaps merely reflecting French literary opinion.

In this light we may also consider an anthology of
that time, French Lyrics of the Nineteenth Century,
by Professor George Neely Henning of George Wash-
ington University, published in 1912 by Ginn and
Company. Professor Henning was not altogether
stodgy either, for he at least included Verlaine, though
he missed out on Rimbaud, to whom he made a passing reference ("gifted but disreputable"); and he
omitted Laforgue. Again, this omission probably reflected French thinking at the time, or even of today,
for as Henri Peyre indicates in his lucid and compre-
hensive essay in the present volume, Laforgue has
never received the extended treatment in France that
he deserves: "The timidity of French scholars is in this
case inexplicable."

The critics in the present volume, chiefly Americans,
are not timid in their assessments and, as I suggested
in the opening sentence of this Preface, their exploration of Laforgue is a many-sided one. Warren Ramsey,
the editor, discusses the individual essays in his Introduction, so I will speak of them here in only a general
way. The comparative method is often of value, and it
is noticeably so in this book; we find Laforgue exam-
ined in the perspective of Baudelaire and Mallarmé
and, in quite a different way, discussed along with
Beckett. And several interesting biographical sections
occur, one of them including new information about
Laforgue's English wife, material supplied by her
great-nephew. Laforgue was a significant ancestor of
much that is good in recent poetry, but he also is an
important author in his own right. The present book
deals valuably with both these aspects of Laforgue; he
will deservedly gain in stature from it.

HARRY T. MOORE

Southern Illinois University
August 16, 1968

Notes on Contributors

MALCOLM COWLEY's recently published *Think Back on Us . . .* gave some indication of how many French writers he discussed, together with Americans with whom he is more frequently associated, while literary editor of *The New Republic* during a crucial decade. Along with such well known books as *Exile's Return, After the Genteel Tradition, The Stories of F. Scott Fitzgerald, The Faulkner-Cowley File* he has published translations of works by Valéry, Gide, Barrès and Radiguet.

CLIVE WARWICK LEE, called up for two years of service in the British Army, spent most of his time in the Suez Canal Zone. On his return he went to Oxford and is an M.A. in theology. Curate of a suburban parish in S.E. London, he has also written an essay on Charles Williams.

RAYMOND POGGENBURG has recently published a paper on Baudelaire and Wallace Stevens and is currently at work on a Baudelaire chronology as well as on a critical preface to and translations from the poetry of Jean-Jacques Celly. An editor of the *Bulletin Baudelairien,* he is Associate Professor of French and Chairman of his department at Vanderbilt University.

HENRI PEYRE, whose many books include a notable study of the nineteenth-century poet-hellenist Louis Ménard, and who has never ceased to inquire into the nature of Classicism, has recently published *Paul Valéry, prose et vers,* with a critical introduction on that most classical of twentieth-century French poets. *Connaissance de Baudelaire, Pensées de Baudelaire, Baudelaire: a Collection of Critical Essays* and the critical commentary on Laforgue in *The Poem Itself* are only a few of Mr. Peyre's other writings having a bearing on his essay here. He is Sterling Professor of French at Yale.

LEO WEINSTEIN'S most recent book is a study of Hippolyte Taine. He is also the author of *The Metamorphoses of Dom Juan*, and, with Jean-Pierre Baricelli, of *Ernest Chausson: the Composer's Life and Works*. Professor of French at Stanford, he has also edited *The Age of Reason: the Culture of the Seventeenth Century*.

WILLIAM JAY SMITH'S *Selected Writings of Jules Laforgue* revealed a special interest on the part of a distinguished American poet. Author of four books of poetry, among them *Celebration at Dark*, and several volumes of children's verse, he has also translated (as *Poems of a Multimillionaire*) Valéry Larbaud's *Poésies de A. O. Barnabooth*. Consultant in poetry to the Library of Congress for 1968–69, he is Professor of English at Hollins College.

ROBERT GREER COHN is the author of three books on Mallarmé—*L'Oeuvre de Mallarmé: Un Coup de Dés* in particular being one that changed readers' minds and critics' views—of *The Writer's Way in France* and many critical essays. Now Professor of French at Stanford, he was the founding editor of *Yale French Studies*.

HASKELL M. BLOCK, author of *Mallarmé and the Symbolist Drama*, has written widely on modern French literature and on critical concepts of long standing. He has edited collections of essays devoted to literary symbolism and has coedited *The Creative Vision: Modern European Writers on Their Art* and *Masters of Modern Drama*. He is Professor of Classics and Comparative Literature at Brooklyn College.

PETER BROOKS, whose study of eighteenth-century French fiction, *The Novel of Worldliness*, is to be published in 1969, has contributed to a number of periodicals. His essay here was written for Professor Renato Poggioli's seminar at Harvard and won the Potter Prize in Comparative Literature. Mr. Brooks is Assistant Professor of French at Yale.

N. CHRISTOPH DE NAGY is the author of *The Poetry of Ezra Pound: the Pre-Imagist Stage* and *Ezra Pound's Poetics and Literary Tradition; the critical decade.* Now Professor of American literature at the University of Berne, he teaches the same subject at the University of Basel.

ERIKA OSTROVSKY is working on a biography of Céline to be published in both French and English, and on a book-length study of the same novelist's style, by way of successors to her recent book, *Céline and His Vision.* She is Associate Professor of French at New York University.

WARREN RAMSEY is perhaps best known for his *Jules Laforgue and the Ironic Inheritance.* He has also written on Mallarmé and, among more recent French poets, on Valéry, Fargue, Apollinaire and Supervielle; on Imagist aims and accomplishment; on Wallace Stevens and on Hart Crane. He is Professor of French and Comparative Literature at the University of California, Berkeley.

Contents

Preface   v

Notes on Contributors   vii

Introduction   xiii
          Warren Ramsey

Laforgue in America: A Testimony   3
          Malcolm Cowley

Leah Laforgue, Her Parents and Family   16
          Clive W. Lee

Laforgue and Baudelaire   26
          Raymond Poggenburg

Laforgue Among the Symbolists   39
          Henri Peyre

Laforgue and His Time   52
          Leo Weinstein

The Moral of the *Moralités*   60
          William Jay Smith

Laforgue and Mallarmé   66
          Robert Greer Cohn

Laforgue and the Theatre   76
          Haskell M. Block

The Rest is Silence: Hamlet as Decadent   93
          Peter Brooks

The Place of Laforgue in Ezra Pound's Literary
  Criticism   111
                        N. Christoph de Nagy

Jules Laforgue and Samuel Beckett: A Rapprochement   130
                        Erika Ostrovsky

Phryne, or More Than One Right Word   146
                        Warren Ramsey

Notes   163

Chronicle   178

Bibliography   183

Index   188

Introduction

Better than anyone else of his time except perhaps
Remy de Gourmont, who had longer to demonstrate
his capacity, Jules Laforgue seems to have been able
to set other literary minds free to go their separate
ways. His verse was formative for the young T. S. Eliot: something like that direct influence which Eliot
took pains to define and defend was at work. His
writings have, moreover, been catalyzing for some
who made no discernible attempt to capture a Laforguian tone or manner. The poet and his work will
be studied from several points of view in the following essays, but their authors will point to no more
interesting trait than a curious power to break whatever spell proved most inhibiting to a beginning
writer.

Of course, Laforgue chose his epoch with his customary rare foresight (as he might have said). By
the time his poems and tales came to be read rather
widely a post-World-War restlessness was in the air.
Among the English-speaking, at least, certain natural
themes of poetry had been regarded with more solemnity than seriousness. In countries which some
said were coming of age, much talent languished for
lack of pointing up or straightening out.

A French poet dead at twenty-seven had possessed
his own set of keys to the corridor leading from the

overstatement that discourages to the understatement that solicits. If a writer simply stops when he feels eloquence welling up within him—if he says, in one way or another, a little less rather than a little more —will the reader not feel impelled to round out, to fill in, for himself? Will he not become a kind of partner in creation and the poem less a thing of black marks on gradually yellowing paper, less "a sheaf of dust," as Hart Crane called one of his poems? Laforgue came to be of this opinion, after a time of making his verses as round as any Parnassian's—or Edwardian's.

His discovery of poetic understatement was, of course, a re-discovery. But it was made at a decisive time by one whose sense of genres and of the rhetorical resources of his language was keen, whose apparent blurring of the one and underplaying (or patent overplaying) of the other were all the more significant. A rhetorical tradition was running strong when Laforgue began to write. It was refined, but not essentially changed, by his immediate elders. Paul Bourget, one of these elders, seems to have been somewhat bewildered by the later works of one whom he, more than anyone else, had encouraged to think for himself and speak with his own voice. Mallarmé was another elder, whom Laforgue all but venerated. Yet Mallarmé's conception and practice of poetry were too different from Laforgue's to permit much more than thoughtful acknowledgment of the *Complaintes*. After the young poet's death came the ripple of general sympathy to which Leo Weinstein refers in this volume, together with more appreciation for the prose tales than for the verse. But Laforgue the writer was long killed with kindness. "Il est mort trop jeune, à vingt-sept ans, pour qu'on puisse le juger; on l'aime," said Gourmont, not foreseeing that a work uncanonical by his standards would one day suggest fresh solutions to problems of expression.

In the meantime much attention would be paid to the quality of Laforgue's temperament, the rareness of his sensitivity, and kindred subjects. This was understandable and even illuminating provided that the Laforguian mind was not oversimplified, made to appear crystal-clear, Gaspard-Hauser-like. One of the contributions to this volume, Erika Ostrovsky's, has the merit of suggesting that there was a darker side to the Laforguian moon. Eclipses, negations may have been exorcised by fairly familiar literary terms and attitudes at first; this was not the case during the later years in Germany.

As an artist Laforgue borrowed several changing shapes, some of the more readily recognizable being those of the poet gaining creative power through sacrifice, à la Fénelon's Philoctetes; the Rousseauesque stroller entirely reconciled with nature; the innocent of Romantic folksong; the clownlike figure only once removed from funambulesque theatre, carnival, or street-corner.

By figures of the last two groups—*pauvres jeunes hommes* at some decisive point in thoroughly miserable existences, husbands more or less outraged, pure-hearted provincials in Paris, pierrots starched and proper, pierrots in autumnal or lunar landscapes, knights-errant firmly withstanding the wiles of the infernal feminine—Laforgue is deservedly remembered. As also for the *complainte* form, the poem only one step away from the *complainte populaire* of September carnival or empty August street of his returns to Paris beginning in 1882. In his *Complaintes* he first broke with his too-literary past. In such poems, around such characters, a little *commedia dell' arte* of his own, the tones he was searching for began to come clear. We have only to bear in mind that this willful primitivism of form and substance represents, strange as this may at first appear, a later stage in an artist's precocious development. The author's personality no longer shines steadily forth from the middle of the page. He is manipulating forms with considerable objectivity.

For insights into what Laforgue himself was like we must turn to transparent early writings, with their record of much intellectual distance traversed; to those of his letters in which he has not yet learned reticence; to occasional personal revelations in the several notebooks that have been preserved; to a contemporary's account of his dreamlike balance when he first arrived in Berlin, the "heredities" that sometimes shattered it, his nervous need for company. We can turn, in this volume, to the Rev. Clive Lee's essay.

Leah Lee Laforgue's great-nephew is mainly concerned with dispelling confusion about her family background. He does this by an account, circumstantial and fascinating, of life as it was in a middle-class English household of the time. Despite family storms that drove Leah off to Germany, her recollections may well have hastened Jules' departure from palace annexes, summer resorts, and hotel rooms— may have intensified his desire to be, as he put it, "less like a parcel," to "install himself in an existence."

How early did he meet Leah—"as tall as you or I, but very thin and very English," as William Jay Smith has translated a letter breaking the news to his sister, "decidedly English, with her reddish brown hair, a red you simply can't imagine and one I wouldn't have believed existed until I saw it, pale skin, thin neck, and eyes . . ." This suggests the glimpse Andromeda catches of herself in her mirror-pool among the rocks. It recalls Syrinx slipping away from Pan in another of the *Moralités*, a figure glimmering through a number of later poems and tales. And some not so late . . .

The letter of September, 1886, just quoted from, tells of having gone to Leah for English lessons the previous January. Her address is, however, jotted down on a page of Laforgue's Agenda for 1883. At what point did "l'illustre R.," an otherwise unidentified personage of the Court, lose her ascendancy and a woman of a quite different type, "une petite Adrienne au bon coeur, aux longs cils, au juvénile et éphémère sourire," take her place? The question has often been asked, never answered, and we are duly grateful for Mr. Lee's conclusion: Jules almost certainly knew Leah long before 1886, probably meeting her at court.

Coming after much longer acquaintance than has previously been known or his "sisterly letter" (as it has been called) to Marie would suggest, his courtship appears in a different light. His decision, to return to Paris with a wife whose consumption was only a little less advanced than his own, seems less impulsive, more significant.

Despite a heavy cold and fever that dogged him during the last three months of 1886, there were some reasons for Laforgue to be optimistic. Life at the German Court had become a timely subject in France. He had been asked to edit a German number of a French magazine, *L'Illustration*, had even sketched a book about Berlin in his mind, had ruled out the possibility of a pension from the Empress so that he would feel freer to write it. The portions of his eventual *Berlin, la Cour et la Ville* which appeared in four numbers of the *Figaro* literary supple-

ment during 1887 are both vivid and largely free of
the Goncourtesque mannerisms which date much of
the prose of the period. Neither his second book of
poems nor his verse play, both of which appeared in
1886, neither his prose tales nor his translations from
Walt Whitman nor even his truly epoch-making
poems in free verse—all of which appeared in Gustave
Kahn's *Vogue* in that same year of magnificent early
harvest—were likely to nourish their man. But his
Chroniques Parisiennes of 1887 helped at least a
little toward that end. However much he chose to
rewrite things that meant much to him, the fact is
that Laforgue *wrote* with considerable ease. Other
creative writers, without his apprenticeship as an art
critic, had somehow managed to survive.

From the early days of January, however, after his
marriage in London on the last day of the year, he
was obliged to hope that friends would come to see
him at 8, rue de Commaille, would understand that
he found even short walks exhausting. "We have a
good fire, a handsome lamp, good tea in the tea
service that the Empress gave me," he wrote to his
sister in January, after telling of his financial straits
and illness. The china tea service, it would seem from
Mr. Lee's article, had been given to Leah and him
together. His sickness and other difficulties were only
beginning.

No one understood very well for a while, to judge
from his repeated and agonized appeals for advances
on his *chroniques*, for loans. Then, rather suddenly,
his friends did understand, and events are relieved by
generous payments for articles, some of them for an
imaginary periodical.

"Wish me a day just a bit warm," he wrote to
Ephrussi in June, as a long cold spring dragged on,
"or a whole series of them if possible." Yet he man-

aged to finish *Berlin, la Cour et la Ville* by the first of July. He wrote to Marie about "un redoublement de maladie"—and his certainty that he would be leaving Paris by the end of September, probably for North Africa, since the indispensable job would be difficult to obtain in Pau. It was late in July when the publisher declined *Berlin,* unless what Laforgue called "grotesque conditions" were satisfied; he immediately started looking for another publisher. On August 2 he tells Marie of his coughing fits, which now last half the night, as their father's did toward the end. The outcome will be entirely different in his case, he is confident, because he is in the hands of Paul Bourget's physician. The summer turned very hot. He admitted that he took too many of his pills, which contained opium and put him to sleep. But he found that if he spent the night propped up in a chair he could breathe more easily. He assented tersely, in spaces Edouard Dujardin had left in his letter, to final suggestions for the *Moralités légendaires.* On August 10 he inquired by postcard what the terms would be for a two weeks' stay at Versailles for Leah and himself.

He died on August 20, a few days after his twenty-seventh birthday. Kathleen Lee, who came from England to be with her sister, here adds her testimony concerning the perfunctoriness with which one of the least expensive of funeral cortèges ground its way through dismally poor quarters toward Bagneux Cemetery. But it should be remembered that the handful of mourners included most of those who had seen Laforgue through his last months. Perhaps they took a realistic view of superfluous trappings for the funeral of a *pauvre jeune homme* who had been looking at death with great simplicity and steadiness for a long time.

Le petit personnage, whose coughing had been one of Jules' chief reasons for leaving Berlin, died not in Menton, as has been too often written, but in St. Peter's Home, Kilburn, less than a year later.

Events had colored, matured, and truncated a life work. A sense of the weight of external factors, of all that remains intractable to individual will and effort, had pervaded a life. This is traceable to the physical sciences of the time, whose conclusions Laforgue incorporated into deadly earnest early poems; to the biological sciences, especially as filtered through the mind of Charles Henry, close friend, frequent correspondent, future physiologist; to early sociologists. It derived from historians and critics who studied works of the aesthetic imagination in the reflected light of the sciences. Laforgue was to challenge aesthetic criteria which he heard Taine develop in his Beaux-Arts lectures—stability and beneficence in the work of art—chiefly by according more importance to the unstable, the transitory. He attached, that is to say, more significance to a work's moment in historical time than did Taine himself. Meanwhile he retained his need, born of temperament and aggravated by experience, to believe. He had lost one faith only to acquire another, ascetic Buddhism. Whatever the merits of this latter, it left him even more open than before to vague but powerfully felt attitudes of resignation expressed by writers who haunt his early style. Finally he half-borrowed, half-invented another faith, obedience to which involved surrender, illusory at least, of individual will to a creative Unconscious. Those phenomena of celestial physics, of group or individual behavior which the scientifically inclined accepted simply as facts, those linkings in a causal chain of supposed facts which Taine laid down with such rhetorical finality, found in Laforgue a quite un-sociological sort of mind. Natural phenomena retained, for him, a certain awesome influence which required all the ingenuity of the creative Unconscious to keep under control. He was all the more free to take both phenomena and ordering principle with his own kind of seriousness because they had new and rather impressive names. He was free to struggle within a web of necessity freshly woven out of old materials—and the last year of his life has its more than ordinary significance.

For Raymond Poggenburg, Laforgue was the modern in search of identity, hence impatient with alleged artifices of his craft. The special resonance of his poetry arises from "our common experiences in conflict with our uncommon longings." That should go far toward explaining Laforgue's emphasis on the rôle of tonal variety in Baudelaire. None better than he, certainly, can say why "Andromaque, je pense à vous . . ." is so effective a beginning for "Le Cygne," a poem partly about a dusty everyday city but mostly about our common experiences in conflict with our uncommon longings. The frequent Baudelairean echoes which Mr. Poggenburg detects in Laforgue's early verse remind us of the vantage point from which he viewed Baudelaire. He was close enough to have had to grapple with him as a fellow-craftsman, far enough away to have some perspective. We can almost forget that those remarkable notes for an essay on Baudelaire are only notes, after all, and the youthful critic might have had second thoughts. When he finds Baudelaire lacking in metaphysical anguish, for example . . . does this mean that Baudelaire's poetry reveals less cleavage between immaterial and material, between concept and image, than Laforgue's? Does it, on the other hand, suggest that Baudelaire was undismayed by the breadth of possible choices, by the burden of freedom? Most modern readers would answer affirmatively to the first question, negatively to the second. Yet Laforgue's notes take us closer to the center of Baudelaire's world than we would otherwise have penetrated. They present a poet who to his critic's mind has great qualities and definite shortcomings—nothing like his present-day reputation—and several serious rivals, notably Verlaine, Corbière, and Rimbaud. They light up the bases of Baudelaire's modern reputation, his modern vocabulary and subject matter, his candor in admitting, as Romantic predecessors had not, the existence of evil, the force of negation, which last Mr. Poggenburg finds to be a theme of Laforgue's *Derniers Vers.*

As Leo Weinstein notes in a background article, 1876 was the year of the third *Parnasse Contemporain.* It was also the year when Charles Laforgue moved with his wife and eleven children to Paris, having the education of his two eldest sons in mind. Jules was probably less aware of the third *Parnasse Contemporain* than of the sights and sounds of Paris but undoubtedly more interested in it than the program of studies toward the *baccalauréat.* The latest *Parnasse . . .* was not a collection bringing the art of poetry into fresh focus, but one to which very good poets indeed, some on the eve of greater discovery, contributed verse of excellent texture. With the Parnassians, Laforgue shared a passion for delineating objects, for making the reader see, which would be one of his chief claims to attention in the twentieth century. He also inherited from the Parnassians—in his early, unoriginal efforts—a taste for the decorous subject, the heroic tone.

Between two crests of accomplishment, French

poetry seemed to be hesitating, gathering its forces together. Laforgue, painfully unsure of himself and his course, hesitated too. The influence of the other arts was no abstraction. His brother was a Beaux-Arts student, Jules himself sketched, compulsively and revealingly, in the margins of many of his manuscripts. His first job was as editorial assistant to the art historian Charles Ephrussi.

Not even the *baccalauréat* pursued as Pan pursued Syrinx could destroy his commitment to ideas. He wanted to renew the themes of poetry. Two waves of German idealism converged in his private kind of Buddhism. Schopenhauer's idealism assumed a new importance in France about 1880, as Mr. Weinstein points out. So, following its translation into French, did Hartmann's *Philosophy of the Unconscious*. From another direction, also noted by Mr. Weinstein, came Herbert Spencer's feeling for the impenetrability of ultimate causes, and a way of looking at society as an organism.

Some of the worst and best of Laforgue's uncertainties were over by the time Gustave Kahn met him at the *Club des Hydropathes*, where acknowledged successors of Baudelaire declaimed verses from whose "naturalisms" Laforgue dissociated himself a shade too vehemently, citing Bourget's dictum that poetry should be to life what a concert of perfumes is to a bed of flowers. Kahn left a little Impressionistic vignette of him as he was that day: book in hand, somewhat too neatly dressed for the occasion, eager and ill-assured, with that hint of the struggling young curate about him which was to persist all during his years in that prosperous parish which was the German court. He was closer to those whom Huysmans had yet to incarnate in the central figure of his *A Rebours*, those solitary admirers of Silver Latin who accepted the epithet "Decadent" without a murmur.

He was to find his *note aiguë*, as he called it, in-dependently and very much alone, in Germany in 1882. At least three years, that is, before the declared principles of Symbolism crystallized around Mallar-mé's poetry. And Laforgue's poetry is not in the least like Mallarmé's. He writes discursively. His language is often direct and spare, fixing, naming objects in the simplest terms. Sometimes he comes deliberately short of the mark, deflating high themes in burlesque. Elsewhere, something unmistakably workaday—his cherished *quotidien*—will be treated with mock gran-deur, heroic-comic inflation, a style that purposely overshoots the target. He can depict with a deft mini-mum of strokes, like Pound and the Anglo-American *Imagistes* who admired and learned from him. De-spite ballad-like snatches and cadences that obsess the memory he was not particularly interested in the pure music, the pure dynamics of language. Nor, as in the case of the *Imagistes*, again, and of Max Jacob, do his real gifts lie in that direction.

Was he a Symbolist, then, in either the historical sense or in the sense of several twentieth-century poets who have intrinsic qualities in common with Mallarmé? Contributors to this volume take differing views. Henri Peyre, tracing with great knowledge and skill Laforgue's literary lineage and pointing to pro-longations of his work, nevertheless places him firmly within the Symbolist Movement. Leo Weinstein, meanwhile, makes a point that cannot be overlooked. Laforgue's moment of self-discovery lay somewhere between the so-called Decadents—not a good name for poets and prose-writers who flourished about 1880 —and Symbolists. He was an idealist without a well-marked destination; his idealism was of a less pure aesthetic alloy than Mallarmé's. He resorted to irony as an alternative to self-pity, and that might be forgiven in a Symbolist—though his use of irony suggests earlier poets, especially Musset and Heine—but he also has recourse to humor, and the true Symbolists never forgot Verlaine's prescription of *le rire impur*.

On the other hand, we find Mallarmé (whose permissiveness as a *chef d'école* Mr. Weinstein deplores, but was that not a rather admirable trait in one who was the guide and conscience of a complex international movement?) calling Laforgue's stories "the Voltaire tales of Symbolism." And Robert Greer Cohn finds Laforgue associating Mallarmé with the creative Unconscious, with the ideal Buddhist sage, with the poetic style that would give the final twist to the neck of eloquence—with whatever mattered most to him at a given time, in short. Mr. Cohn would range Laforgue among the Symbolists broadly understood as those who were "late Romantic in emotional powers and classic in precision of aesthetic form." He argues for the significance of the matrix-work, the original conception at once foreshadowing and dwarfing works actually brought to completion. Both Mallarmé and Laforgue had such prophetic books in mind at one time. Mr. Cohn is able to point, besides, to common denominators in individual poems. Less convincingly, he suggests resemblances between thin concepts in the rambling discourse pronounced by Laforgue's bluestocking, Salomé, and ideas given luminous density in two of Mallarmé's poems. Whether or not we agree that the two men belonged to a fellowship of minds, whether or not we can see much resemblance between vague preliminary conceptions and finished works emerging from the ardent search for form, the *Derniers Vers* deserve a description once given to Eliot's poetry. They weave a "music of ideas."

Mallarmé was glad to claim Laforgue's prose tales for Symbolism. They have been highly praised from time to time since. And yet humor is precarious and parody can be downright dangerous, particularly when gods and demigods like Flaubert are its object. Almost to the end of a much buffeted existence Laforgue preserved streaks of what we are pleased to call "immaturity." These are more evident in his prose (except the last written tale, "Pan et la Syrinx") than in his verse. Nor have we Americans usually read Giraudoux at an early age, to give us a taste for mythology irreverently brought up to date. Altogether, it is well to have an excellent poet of the mid-century, William Jay Smith, to interpret the *Moralités*, continuing here the sensitive commentary begun in his *Selected Writings of Jules Laforgue*. "What he says in the entire book," writes Mr. Smith, "is that all the past—history, myth and legend—exists everywhere and for all of us: we are in it, and it is in us." Something survives "destruction of the hero." Individual consciousness reconstructs the myth, and it was Laforgue's appreciation of this fact that interested James Joyce. Mr. Smith also comments on color symbolism, key themes, and the gradual transformation of an attitude exalting art for art's sake to one justifying art for life's sake.

One essay deals with Laforgue the incipient playwright, another with his handling of a dramatic archetype, another points a parallel between his "Hamlet" and a product of twentieth-century *Nouveau Théâtre*. This is as it should be, in view of the deeper nature of the body of poetry and prose forever in movement toward dramatic form. But dramatic form is not necessarily theatrical form. Laforgue's only completed play failed resoundingly when produced four years after his death. Was this merely the predictable flurry of resistance met with by an original work? Could a Laforguian theatre, a poet's theatre not unlike Musset's, in which the comic has its function, have crossed over into the realm where plays are really played? Haskell Block, known for authoritative studies of the Symbolist theatre, adduces significant facts: Laforgue's sheer delight in performance, including circuses and their clowns; his deepseated need to communicate with an audience; the genesis of the *complainte* form, out of public recitals. Mr. Block also notes a gain in dramatic power in "Hamlet," prose tale though it be, and two adaptations of this piece suggest that men of the theatre concur. Peter Brooks mentions another poet-dramatist, Yeats, almost of an age with Laforgue, whose later career indicates that a poet with enough rhetorical power need not always be unlucky in the theatre.

Mr. Brooks is not merely concerned with "the latent lord unable to become, boyish shadow of us all"—the late nineteenth-century idea of Hamlet and the quietus Laforgue makes thereof. A cult of sterility—of purity—found a natural center in Laforgue's *pudeur*. What Mr. Brooks says incidentally about Mallarmé's and Joyce's understanding of Hamlet is also interesting. Mallarmé's closest approach to the myth, "Igitur," is sketchy, and Villiers' *Axël* is far too much the prefabricated triangle. Laforgue's "Hamlet" offers the amplest evidence of that gallery of mirrors which *Hamlet* set before the Symbolist mind.

Erika Ostrovsky discovers similarities of setting in "Hamlet" and Samuel Beckett's *Fin de Partie*. These might have a common origin in some collective symbolism. She suggests kinship of sensibility—and in that area judgment is a hazardous cast of the dice.

Yet she manages to suggest an aspect of Laforgue which must have made many flinch because virtually no one has written about it: a certain harshness of negation lying just beyond highly elaborated imagery of sterility, just on the poet's side of discarded fragments where imagery is insufficiently worked out. These latter—rough blocks of poems apparently beginning with some fresh glimpse of industrial ugliness or Zolaesque city poverty—do not quite come off. Swift responses to things seen, they are staccato, substantival, asyntactical without Rimbaud's visionary intensity, which fused atoms together. And they are a part of Laforgue's work necessary to full understanding of the whole.

His theatre, had it materialized, would have shaded away from representation of character toward presentation of mood, like other theatrical mood-pieces of the time, rather than toward the grotesque of twentieth-century *Nouveau Théâtre*. But his theatre did not materialize. Nor was he a storyteller in any usual sense, excluding as he did from the *Moralités légendaires* the two pieces most likely to place him in a contemporary mainstream of psychological realism. He had long since taken his leave of a less psychological, more lyrical kind of realism in *Stéphane Vassiliew*. And it is unlikely that he would have returned to his unfinished Stendhalian novel begun in Germany, which he called *Un Raté*. Clearly, he was in search of something else, the Nietzschean "arrows of longing for the other shore" were keen. Or, to adapt slightly the words of a poet who owed much to him, Jules Supervielle, he was the man whose thoughts reach out toward something else, the man who spends his life thinking of something else. And because his poetry, the best of it, is lacking in familiar magnificences, it has often invited the word "minor," which does not account for positive qualities. It does not, for example, explain why Prufrock could hardly have existed without Laforgue's self-deprecating personages and certainly would not have been the same without the fluid free-verse meters of the *Derniers Vers*.

No one is likely to exhaust the mystery of the generative force released by a fragile handful of poems and tales chanced upon, often at odd times and in unlikely places, by creative men. But Christoph de Nagy brings us closer to the heart of our matter by his 1962 study of the place of Laforgue's writing—including "Salomé," curiously enough—among Ezra Pound's touchstones. He tells how Pound made his sampling of the poems available to young American poets in a memorable issue of *The Little Review*, how he invented a critical term to cope with "the dance of the intellect among words." And Malcolm Cowley, who at a decisive point read Laforgue as a young poet reads, responding in his own poetry, brings us still closer to understanding. Mr. Cowley's place as a critic of French (and much other) literature has been won by what the Existentialists used to call *une pensée vécue*. No one else could have spoken quite as authoritatively about meanings of Laforgue for American poets, or conveyed in such a lively style the essential of Eliot's and Pound's and Crane's encounters. What was it about Laforgue that caught the attention of young American poets? Mr. Cowley answers fully, with suitable illustrations from his own poems.

The editor is particularly grateful to the American Philosophical Society for a grant enabling him to consult manuscripts at the Bibliothèque Jacques Doucet of the University of Paris and to complete his introduction with due attention to points made elsewhere in this volume. Laforgue and his work lend themselves to scrutiny by a group. His mind was drawn—or torn—in many directions by the complex variety of a decade to which he reacted with a swift and often topical precision. Special competences are needed in order to penetrate, to interpret fully. We would have wished it larger, ". . . notre fête / Très simple de chanter l'absence du poète . . ." And to some who could not participate we owe much-appreciated encouragement.

Acknowledgments are due to the editors of *The Sewanee Review*, in whose Winter 1963 issue Malcolm Cowley's essay appeared in slightly different form.

WARREN RAMSEY

Jules Laforgue
    Essays on a Poet's Life and Work

Laforgue in America: A Testimony
Malcolm Cowley

Deponent states: My name is Malcolm Cowley. I was born in 1898 and I am by profession a literary critic and historian. In 1929 I published a first book of poems, *Blue Juniata*. It was divided into five sections, arranged in a roughly autobiographical order, and each section was preceded by an explanatory note intended to set the tone of what followed. The note preceding one of the sections, called "The Adolescent," read in part:

> After the war, we drifted to New York, to the district south of Fourteenth street, where one could occupy a hall bedroom for two or three dollars weekly and rent the unfurnished top floor of a rickety dwelling for thirty dollars a month. There were two schools among us: those who painted the floors black (they were the last of the aesthetes) and those who did not paint the floors. Our college textbooks and the complete works of Jules Laforgue gathered dust on the mantelpiece among a litter of unemptied ash-trays.

Two questions that might strike a reader are, first, why and how the works of Jules Laforgue (then in four volumes published by the Mercure de France) found their way to a mantelpiece in an old brick rat-infested house on I remember it was Bedford Street, in the realm of the Hudson Dusters, and second, what influence they had on the poems that some of us were writing in those days. By "us" I mean the apprentice writers of 1920, those who had interrupted their college years by enlisting in the armed services or, more likely, in the unarmed American Ambulance Service attached to the French armies. Now we were home again, and Laforgue must have stood for something in the civilian lives we hoped to lead.

What that something was and how it got into our lives is a story that goes back to a time shortly before we were born. At Harvard in the early 1890's, there were several gifted poets all of whom died young; collectively they deserved the name that Yeats applied to his friends of the same age in London: the Tragic Generation. William Vaughn Moody and George Cabot Lodge were members of the group, but the best of them, I think, was Trumbull Stickney, who was born in 1874 and died at the age of thirty. Most of those Harvard poets had a particular sense of life that was based partly on Greek classicism and partly on French Symbolism. It is strictly in character that Stickney was not only the first American to be granted a *Doctorat ès lettres* by the Sorbonne but also chose as a subject for his French dissertation "Axioms in Greek Poetry from Homer to Euripides." His poems showed a similar combination of Greek learning with a number of qualities cultivated by French poets of his own time, including the use of bold metaphors controlled by irony; and the combination reappears, if not so strikingly, in other poets of the group.

After the undergraduate years of the Tragic Generation, there was always an undercurrent of interest at Harvard in French Symbolist poetry. The interest was kept alive partly through the efforts of an instructor long remembered by his students, though almost lost to academic history; his name was Pierre La Rose. I don't know whether T. S. Eliot met La Rose when

Eliot was an undergraduate in the class of 1910, but at any rate he met others familiar with the Symbolist poets. He carried on the tradition of the 1890's, and by his junior year he was contributing poems to the *Harvard Advocate* that were written in an unmistakably Laforguian manner. The story continues with Eliot's early years in London, when he was unhappily teaching school and, in his leisure time, writing the poems of his "Prufrock" period. In 1914 he met Ezra Pound, who introduced him to many French poets he had not read, or had not read attentively, but in one case the introduction was reversed: it was Eliot who taught Pound to admire Laforgue.

Pound's new admiration was expressed at some length in an article he wrote for the February 1918 issue of the *Little Review*; he used most of the issue to present a number of French Symbolist poets, including Laforgue, with sweeping comments and with samples of their work in the original. In those days Pound was a marvelous impresario, even if he did not always grasp the best elements of the poets he was presenting to a new audience. In the case of Laforgue, for example, if Pound came to a passage he did not understand —either in the poems or in one of the *Moralités légendaires*, which he translated in another article—he simply omitted the difficult sentence or stanza or paragraph. But he had an assured manner that overwhelmed his readers, so that everything he wrote about French poetry—and especially the *Little Review* article in 1918—had a lasting influence on younger American poets.

At that time such poets were appearing in large numbers. Many of them became familiar with Laforgue, in some cases through the Harvard tradition, in some cases through Pound's article, and in some cases from other sources. I cannot remember in what circumstances I first read the poems. Perhaps it was Kenneth Burke who introduced me to Laforgue; Kenneth was making his own explorations of French literature and was spending most of his days at the New York Public Library. Perhaps I discovered Laforgue in 1917, when I was in France with the American Field Service and was buying anthologies of modern French poetry, notably that famous collection by Van Bever and Léautaud, "Poètes d'aujourd'hui," in which young Americans could learn more than they wanted to know about Symbolism. I also think of S. Foster Damon, who was a graduate student at Harvard from 1914 to 1918 and later an instructor there. A great reader of French poetry, he passed along his discoveries to his roommate, E. E. Cummings, and later to me and John Brooks Wheelwright. However introduced to Laforgue, I read, I was converted, and the four yellow-backed volumes of his work, with not all the pages cut (especially in the *Mélanges posthumes*), stood gathering dust on my mantelpiece, as on many others, among that litter of unemptied ashtrays.[1]

But what was it that most of us saw in Laforgue and tried to reproduce in our own work? I have to admit that most of us read French poems with the help of a dictionary (which we were sometimes too lazy to use), that we were not at the time well versed in the rules of French prosody, and that we often misunderstood what we were reading. Not long ago I found a document that revealed what might be called our typical ignorance. It was Hart Crane's copy of Laforgue, with two stanzas of the "Complainte des Nostalgies Préhistoriques" annotated in Hart's handwriting. Here are the stanzas and the annotations:

> darkens
> *La nuit bruine sur les villes.*
> *Mal repu des gains machinals,*   mechanical gains

On dîne; et, gonflé d'idéal,	swelled with ideals
Chacun sirote son idylle,	each one sighs his idyll
Ou furtive, ou facile.	

Echos des grands soirs primitifs!		
Couchants aux flambantes usines,		factories
Rude paix des sols en gésine,	earth	childbirth
Cri jailli là-bas d'un massif,		
Voluptés à vif!		

The least one can say after reading the notations is that Hart's French vocabulary was not extensive. I wonder if he guessed at the combination of two words in *voluptés*? Possibly he did, for he enjoyed making the same sort of combinations in English. But his translations of the first three "Locutions des Pierrots" were so far from the original poems that he had to apologize in a footnote. "A strictly literal translation of Laforgue" he said, "is meaningless. The native implications of his idiosyncratic style have to be recast in English garments." My own knowledge of French at the time was a little greater than Hart's; after all, I had spent those six months in the American Field Service and had even acquired a *marraine*. Still, there were broad gaps in my learning, as in that of every other young American poet. What puzzles me is how it came about that Laforgue had a deep influence on so many of us, considering that we had to approach him through such a screen of ignorance.

It was probably because there were a few characteristics of his that penetrated the screen. First of all, we were impressed by his subject matter. Most of our reading had been among country poets, and Laforgue seemed new to us partly because he was urban. Moreover, we were young and yearning, and we found it exciting to read a poet who regarded adolescence as a time of life that deserved as much serious attention as any other time. He perfectly expressed our feelings about women (excepting mothers and aunts) when he singularized and rarefied the petticoated multitude into the Eternal Feminine. She, that is, womankind, was at the same time our hope and yearning, our necessity, and the ogress who would lock us in her dungeon. Weak and irresistible, compassionate, pitiless, and perhaps essentially stupid, She would snatch us from our lonely divagations under the moon and make us the daylight prisoners of convention. All this we found in Laforgue, and we also found confirmation of our instinctive notion about the best means of defending ourselves. The best means was a style, a literary attitude applied to life; it was irony, paradox, and a parade of learning. If we laughed at ourselves and Her in the same breath, we should be safe even against tears, even against the heartbroken "Ah! you don't love me!" We could always dream of answering coldly with Lord Pierrot, "The sum of the angles of a triangle, dear heart, is equal to two right angles."

Besides a subject and a strategy, we also found a language in Laforgue. I don't mean that we mastered French, but rather that we sensed another language in his poems for which French was chiefly a mode and a mask. The other language was a new, at the time, amalgam of learned words from philosophy, medicine, and the natural sciences with familiar expressions, street slang, and newspaper phrases beautifully misapplied. Ezra Pound spoke of Laforgue as being the poet who had most highly developed the art of what he called "logopoeia," that is, a playing about with the ordinary meanings of words, and certainly, in those days, a little host of young American poets would have liked to become logopoeists.

Then comes one other characteristic of Laforgue that was striking enough to be perceived through the screen of ignorance. It was the free but singing rhythm of his verse, especially in the *Complaintes*. This might seem a curious thing to say, considering that there have always been learned arguments about the rhythm of French verse and considering that French prosody is based on a syllabic count of the lines and not on accents recurring at more or less regular intervals. But the *Complaintes* are built around popular songs of which the pounding rhythm is suggested by Laforgue's refrains. A transatlantic reader could sense the rhythm, whether or not he was familiar with the song:

> —"Pré*aux des* soirs,
> Christs *des dor*toirs!

> "Tu *t'en* vas *et* tu *nous* lais*ses*,
> Tu *nous* laiss*'s et* tu *t'en* vas,

Hearing the words that echo through my mind after so many years, I realize that I was misplacing the accents in the next two lines. But if I had then known the children's burlesque dirge around which Laforgue was writing variations, I might have found an excuse for my reading the lines, not as French octosyllables, but as English tetrameters:

> Dé*faire* et *refaire ses* tres*ses*,
> Bro*der d'é*ter*nels* canevas."

The chant that we heard, or fancied we heard, in lines like these was something we tried to reproduce in our own verses, where we also used, on occasion, the Laforguian device of a couplet, usually in a different meter, that summarizes or comments upon the preceding stanza:

> —"*Coeurs en prison,*
> *Lentes saisons!*

an effect brilliantly reproduced in J. Alfred Prufrock's

> *I grow old . . . I grow old . . .*
> *I shall wear the bottoms of my trousers rolled.*

Merely as confirmation of these statements, the deponent wishes to place in evidence some of the poems he wrote in the 1920's that reveal the influence of Laforgue or attempt to reproduce some of his qualities in English. Exhibit A might be the first stanza of a poem printed in the *Little Review*, called "After Jules Laforgue." It comes pretty far after him, but the poet might have offered Hart Crane's excuse, that the "native implications of his idiosyncratic style have to be recast in English garments":

> *Sundays in my bedroom staring*
> *Through the broken window pane*
> *I watch the slanting lines of rain*
> *And since I have an empty purse*
> *Turn to philosophy again—*
> > *The world is a potato paring,*
> > *Refuse of the universe,*
> > > *And man excrescent,*
> > > *Adolescent.*

Although the English garments might be better cut, still we have the short couplet rhyming on Latinate words and offered as comment upon the preceding stanza, we have the philosophy that is less cosmic than it sounds, and we have the word "adolescent," a key to much that we found in Laforgue. Exhibit B is part of a poem called "Nocturne," first printed in the *Hound & Horn*. Obviously to us, though not to the young author who wrote it, the poem was inspired by Laforgue's "Complaint of the Pianos One Hears in Residential Streets":

> *Mother has washed the dishes, limped upstairs;*
> *Mother has disappeared into the light;*
> *porches are filled where wicker rocking chairs*
> *creak . . . through the emptiness of night*
> *. . . creak . . . scrape, as if they would repeat*
> *the litany of the daughters of the street:*

"Hamburg steak for dinner, ladders in our hose,
nobody speaks of them, everybody knows;
   meeting me at twilight he handed me a rose:
will he come?"

"Nocturne" is close to the form and spirit of its French model, especially when Laforgue's young man appears at the end of the poem (though not in his disguise of Pierrot) and explains himself to the eternal young woman:

> "*Your folk are stronger than mine,*
>   *being less bold;*
> *your arms are stronger than mine,*
>   *willing to hold;*
> *your faith is stronger than mine,*
>   *founded on lies;*
> *my faith is no longer mine,*
> *but melts away in your eyes,*
> *in the syrup of your eyes.*
> *I can never belong to you.*"
>
> *And she: "It is not true."*
>
> *My words have tapped like pebbles*
> *in the dry well of her mind.*
> *She only smiles and echoes,*
> "*It is not true. You are unkind.*"
> *Or else she answers nothing of the kind.*

Exhibit C is submitted to show how Laforgue's practice encouraged us to experiment with a Latinate vocabulary. The poem here quoted in part was called, quite briefly, "Time":

> *Twilight. And still the clock*
> *ticks viciously at every second;*
> *the minutes stalk*
> *grimly across the field of consciousness;*
> *an hour is a time unreckoned*

precise and categorical
the seconds hammer on the wall.

At their touch the flesh disintegrates:
the mind is a cerebrum, a cerebellum,
dirty gray whorls like a ball of cotton waste,
a bundle of soiled linen, a bale of shoddy.
The seconds drip from a great height,
exploding one by one against the nerves,
against the broken carapace of body;
each second is eroding like the rain
its bit of flesh or deliquescent brain.

The final piece of evidence, Exhibit D, is a poem here printed for the first time. I felt it was a little too juvenile for publication when I wrote it at the age of twenty-one, in that room on Bedford Street where the four dust-covered volumes of Laforgue stared down at me from the mantelpiece. Today I think it has some value as a document surviving from those comparatively innocent years. Even the title is Laforguian:

Variations on a Cosmical Air

Love is the flower of a day,
Love is a rosebud—anyway,
When we propound its every feature
We make it sound like horticulture,
And even in our puberty
We drown love in philosophy.

But I'm coming around in a taxi, honey,
Tomorrow night with a roll of money;
You wanna be ready 'bout ha-past eight.

As celibates we cerebrate
Tonight, we stutter and perplex
Our minds with Death and Time and Sex;
We dream of star-sent, heaven-bent
Plans for perpetual betterment;
Tomorrow morning we shall curse
To find the self-same universe.

Frankie and Johnny were lovers —
Lordy, how those two could love!
They swore to be true to each other,
Just as true as the stars above.

The stars above my attic chamber
Are old acquaintances of mine
And closer now than I remember;
The moon, a last year's valentine,
Coquets with me, though growing fusty;
The Milky Way is pale and dusty;
"Freud is my shepherd, there are no sins,"
Whispers the Virgin to the Twins.

Even the best of friends must part,
Put your money on the dresser before you start.

Before I start let planets break
And suns turn black before I wake
Alone tomorrow in this room;
I want a cosmic sort of broom
To reach the Bear and Sirius even,
Annihilate our ancient heaven,
Or rearrange in other pairs
Those interstellar love affairs,
Finding a mate for everyone
And me, and me, before I'm done.

Ashes to ashes and dust to dust,
Stars for love and love for money;
If the whiskey don't get you the cocaine must,
And I'm coming around in a taxi, honey.

Having submitted these exhibits, I attest and depose
that they constitute, with the preceding statements, a
true record of one poet and his early debt to Laforgue.
It is possible that the debt may have been somewhat
smaller than the exhibits would seem to indicate. In
talking about literary sources, we always run the danger of assuming that because something is *post hoc* —
in this case, post Laforgue — it is also *propter hoc*.
Some of the resemblances are due to the air of the

times, in 1920, and the common perplexities of adolescence. But there *was* an influence, and a great one, and I suspect that several other poets who started writing at about the same time might be willing to offer depositions of much the same nature. Of course the great example of a Laforguian poem in English is "The Love Song of J. Alfred Prufrock," which combines such characteristics as the urban background, the timidly yearning hero (in this case older than Laforgue's beardless Pierrots), the self-protective irony, the bold figures of speech, the mixture of colloquial and academic language, the rhythms that might be those of popular songs, and the rhyming couplets serving as refrains. Besides presenting all those Laforguian elements, "Prufrock" ends with perhaps the most effective use in English or French of a device to which Kenneth Burke gave the name of "tangent ending." Laforgue was fond of the device and apparently discovered it for himself, even if he was not the first to adopt it. Essentially it consists in rounding out a story or a situation, then moving away from it at a tangent, as if, after making a tour of the house, one had found a door that opened on a new landscape. Such a door is what Alfred Prufrock finds after making his tea-time visit and deciding that he will never have courage to confess his yearnings. The episode and the poem seem to be ending together, when suddenly Prufrock dreams of walking on the beach and listening to the mermaids' songs.

> *I have seen them riding seaward on the waves*
> *Combing the white hair of the waves blown back*
> *When the wind blows the water white and black.*
>
> *We have lingered in the chambers of the sea*
> *By sea-girls wreathed with seaweed red and brown*
> *Till human voices wake us, and we drown.*

That is, for me, one of the great moments in twentieth-century English poetry, and I do not think it is equaled by anything in *The Waste Land*, which has dozens of tangents running off in all directions from a circle that is never clearly drawn. Even before *The Waste Land*, but after the period of his Laforguian poems, Eliot had entered a different stage in which, cheered on by Pound, he was trying to reproduce the qualities of other French poets, and notably of Tristan Corbière. Almost all that remains of Laforgue in this so-called "Sweeney" period is the popular songs in "Fragment of an Agon" and the polysyllabic language of "The Hippopotamus."

Pound himself was never deeply influenced by Laforgue, and what he got out of him was hardly the best that the poet had to offer. He seems to have been impressed chiefly by the dexterity in playing with words and by the tone of sophisticated detachment, so that Pound's Laforgue is a *boulevardier* rather than a sensitive adolescent. What Pound most enjoyed was savage wit, and he found more of it in Corbière, as also in Laurent Tailhade, whom he regarded as one of the great. The younger poets who had been influenced by Laforgue also looked for other masters before they were ready to stand alone. He is not particularly admired by the present generation. It remains true, however, that his work helped to change the course of American poetry and that its influence here was based on an instinctive sympathy amounting almost, at the time, to an identity of spirit. That explains why he was a liberating force, in style and form and subject matter. I attest and depose that he encouraged a number of American poets to speak with greater freedom, in voices that later proved to be their own.

Leah Laforgue, Her Parents and Family
Clive W. Lee

Little has been published concerning the family and background of the English girl who married Jules Laforgue, and, with the lively exception of one article,[1] most of that little has been speculative and erroneous. The truth is that Leah Lee Laforgue was never really estranged from her large family. While she was dying of consumption at Saint Peter's Home, Kilburn, at least one of her sisters visited her, and as David Arkell has written, her brother Edgar made the long journey from the north of Scotland to South Devon to conduct her funeral. Until fairly recently many people who knew her well must have been alive. The last two of her sisters have died within the last few years. Now, however, it is almost too late to look for anyone who knew her, and documentary evidence must be relied on to verify and reinforce the information that has reached her nephews and nieces.

In the July 1950 number of *French Studies*, Oxford, R. R. Bolgar confesses that most of what is known about Leah is contained in the letter that Laforgue began to write to his sister Marie on his wedding day, December 31, 1886. (He might have added the letter written on September 8, 1886, announcing his engagement.) Laforgue informed his sister that Leah had told him that she had a brother who was a lawyer in Folkestone, another who was an Army officer in Zululand and another who was a clergyman in New Zealand. Mr. Bolgar only mentions the "clergyman in New Zealand." Unfortunately Laforgue had confused two of the brothers, for in fact Ernest Page Lee was at the time a barrister in New Zealand and Edgar Lee was an Anglican priest in Folkestone. This obviously misled Mr. Bolgar, and he searched Crockford and the Clergy List in vain for a clergyman called Lee in New Zealand at this time and concluded that Leah had invented the professions of her brothers. His suspicions that her capacity for accuracy was somewhat wanting were further aroused when he found that, in the entry of the marriage in the register of Saint Barnabas Church, Kensington, her age is given as twenty-two, while the General Register Office at Somerset House has no record of a Leah Lee born in 1864. However, he found a Leah Mary Lee who was born at Erith in Kent in 1866 and whose father was a blacksmith called Samuel Lee. Mr. Bolgar concluded that this was the Leah he was looking for, and not without reason: in the marriage entry Leah Laforgue's father is also given as Samuel Lee, and he is described, as he was wont to describe himself, as Gentleman. Mr. Bolgar, having decided that the blacksmith's daughter was she who was to become the wife of Jules Laforgue, felt that she was trying to hide her origins from her husband.

Mr. Warren Ramsey saw no reason to doubt Mr. Bolgar's somewhat uneasy conclusions when, in Chapter X of *Jules Laforgue and the Ironic Inheritance* he agreed that Leah "misrepresented more or less innocently when she gave Jules to understand that she had a brother who was a lawyer in Folkestone, another who was a clergyman in New Zealand . . ." and that "she was probably the daughter of a blacksmith . . ." Both Bolgar and Ramsey seek to be kind to Leah and to excuse her from her apparent untruthfulness.

The reason for the incorrect age in the marriage

register remains a mystery, for it seems strange that a woman of twenty-five who is about to marry a man of twenty-six should give her age as twenty-two. Leah may have done so deliberately, but it is not unlikely that William Inch, the verger or parish clerk, or J. H. Greaves, the officiating priest, made the mistake. Laforgue's account of this slovenly ceremony[2] would seem to support this hypothesis. First-hand experience convinces me that such an error is possible. But this is an unimportant point, and documentary evidence leaves no doubt that Leah Laforgue was born and baptized in 1861, the daughter of Samuel and Leah Lee of Teignmouth, in South Devon.

In a letter published in *The Times Literary Supplement* of February 5, 1954, Mr. Bolgar criticizes Mr. Ramsey for making use of what he calls his tentative hypothesis concerning the social origins of Leah Lee and says that evidence has come to light that Leah's references to her brothers were true. By this time he had consulted another relation of Leah's, but even so his information was still erroneous, for he speaks of the lawyer brother in New Zealand ending his life as Minister of Education. In fact, Ernest Page Lee became, in 1920, Minister of Justice, Industries and Commerce, and External Affairs. He was also in control of Police and Prisons, and for a short while Attorney General. In 1922 he lost his seat and although he was returned to Parliament in 1925 he did not reassume his former positions. He again lost his seat in 1928 and retired from public life. He died suddenly in 1932. To make him Minister of Education at the end of his life is, again, a minor error, yet one showing how little real research has been made into Leah's background. A sketch of what is known for certain of Leah's family will not now be out of place.

Leah was one of a family of twelve children, all very

different from one another in their capabilities and disabilities and the balance of both in their separate characters. There is a definite dividing line between those who had completed their basic schooling and were more or less grown up by the time of their mother's death and the younger five, who never quite achieved the intellectual maturity or the adventurous assurance of the elder seven. To a greater or lesser degree the older children all forged ahead, with the exception perhaps of the third son, Herbert. They grew up together and influenced each other and together enjoyed the affluent and strict life of the prosperous Victorian home, where they were encouraged to develop their talents, and achieve the Victorian virtue of being well-bred and what today is sometimes called cultured. They were certainly well educated.

Leah was born in 1861, the sixth child of Samuel and Leah Lee. By this time her father was growing prosperous. He and his wife had laid the foundations of a thriving drapery and ladies' and gentlemen's outfitting business at 7 Regent Street, Teignmouth. This proved so successful that on his retirement after his wife's death in 1883, he felt entitled, as did many Victorian businessmen, to style himself "gentleman," whenever a description was required in any formal document.

Samuel came from yeoman stock farming in the Crediton area in North Devon. He was the son of John Ocock Lee and was born at Zeal Monachorum near Crediton in 1826. His father died in 1832, and it seems that he went to live with a relation in the nearby village of North Tawton and was apprenticed in the drapery trade. Nothing more is known of him until 1853, when on August 27 he married Leah Page of Clyst St. George, near Exeter, the daughter of John Page, who farmed Well and Green's End Farms and in addition was a butcher. In the marriage register Samuel is described as a linen draper of East Teignmouth. It is not known if he already occupied the premises at 7 Regent Street, but he was there by 1861 and it was there that his family lived above the shop at least until 1875. Here his children were born and here the business prospered until it occupied at least the ground floors of several buildings. Soon after 1875 the family moved to "Rosenville," a house in Bank Street, West Teignmouth. The children were now growing up. In 1877 the youngest son, Percival, was born and the eldest child, Fanny, was twenty-three.

For almost a quarter of a century children had been born at more or less regular intervals. A second daughter, Leah, died in infancy, and members of the family have also mentioned twins who, in the early years of the marriage, scarcely saw the light of day before closing their eyes upon it forever. Edgar was born in 1857, Lewis in 1858, Herbert in 1859. Leah, *le petit personnage*, arrived on April 9, 1861. Between 1862 and 1875 came Ernest Page, Kathleen, better known as Kate, Edith, who soon died, and Bertha, Ethel, Arthur, and Warwick. Sixteen children in all, counting the four who died!

Samuel Lee worked hard and he worked his employees and apprentices hard. A few years ago an old lady who had been one of his apprentices remembered having arrived late one morning at a few minutes past eight o'clock to find her master waiting, watch in hand.

As was the custom, the children were looked after by a succession of governesses and nurses while Mrs. Lee worked with her husband and became a driving force in building up the business. It was she who supervised the buying and, to cater to customers who required the highest fashion, made buying expeditions to Paris as well as to London. A photograph taken in Kensington in about 1875 shows her elegantly dressed in a long trailing brocade gown and what appears to be a black lace shawl.

As Samuel was strict and methodical in business, exploiting to the full the capabilities of his employees, so as a father he expected a high standard of achievement from his children. He was prepared to invest his time and money in his business and to spend the fruits of his labor on his children, from whom he demanded obedience and respect. In old age his son Warwick remembered that, as a little boy, he, as a matter of course, made an appointment with his father to solicit the gift of a penny.

Samuel Lee, the draper, wished to be respected as a gentleman and accordingly his children were educated in the manner befitting their father's claim. Little is known of the early education of the elder children. It is recorded that Ernest was at school at Cheltenham and it may be supposed that the other older brothers were there too, but there is no real evidence. Their subsequent careers suggest a good education. It is believed that the girls were at the Maynard School, Exeter, but unfortunately this cannot be verified. The building which contained the papers relating to the earlier days of the school was destroyed in the one-night blitz on Exeter during the War. Arthur, and probably Warwick, and perhaps Percy also, went to Thorn Park School, Teignmouth, until the home broke up after the death of Mrs. Lee and Samuel moved from Teignmouth.

This great crisis and turning point in the life of the family came on September 17, 1883, when the mother of this large family died at the age of fifty-one. For two months she suffered some internal disease culminating in a hemorrhage which went on for five days until she died in the arms of her son Herbert, leaving a grief-stricken family. Herbert had gone to New Zealand with his elder brother Lewis in about 1880, but had

come home when his mother's illness was known to be
fatal. By this time Lewis was probably in South Africa,
where he eventually settled as a gold prospector, since
by 1886 Leah was able to describe him to Jules as an
officer in Zululand. It seems that he returned to England sooner than Herbert, joined the army, and was
posted to South Africa, where he later abandoned his
army career for a more lucrative occupation. He, the
second son, was twenty-five when his mother died,
while the youngest child, Percy, was only six.

Meanwhile Ernest, having been articled to a firm of
West of England solicitors in 1880, completed his
articles with their London agent and read for his degree at London University. At the time of his mother's
death he may not have been living at home. Edgar,
who had grown up to be generous, affectionate, and
somewhat eccentric, had been greatly impressed by
the life and worship of the Church of Saint Nicholas,
Shaldon, near Teignmouth, where he had worshipped
and from 1878 until 1880 had been voluntary organist.
Like his brother Herbert, he was highly proficient as
an organist, having developed a passion for keyboard
instruments from a very early age. By the time of his
mother's death he was well advanced in his training
for the Anglican priesthood and was to receive his
degree from London University in 1884. The eldest
daughter, Fanny, and Leah, who was now twenty-two,
were also at home, as were all the younger children.
Kathleen was nineteen. Bertha had her fifteenth birthday only a week previously, when her mother was
obviously dying, and her family was too distracted to
pay any attention to her, except for Leah who, to
comfort her sister, took off her bracelet and gave it to
her. The other children were all younger than Bertha.

The family submerged itself in deep mourning and
Samuel became so demented with grief that the funeral arrangements had to be taken out of his hands.

It was now arranged that Leah and Kate should take over the running of the home but this arrangement was abandoned when Louisa Crawford wrote to Samuel and offered her services as housekeeper. She had formerly been employed by him as a governess and her offer was accepted. Within a year Samuel married her. His grief for his first wife was spent and he paid her the compliment of marrying again. His elder children did not see it this way and were outraged. Terrible scenes resulted. Mrs. Louisa Lee was forced to keep to her bedroom while her step-children were commanded by their father to address her as "my dear"!

The situation at this time was clearly intolerable to the whole family, and although exact chronology is not possible, the events of late 1884 and 1885 can be noted.

Samuel and Louisa Lee, joined by her sister, Mrs. Ellen Drysdale, removed with the five younger children to Derby and thence to Bedford. It is not known when they left Derby to go to Bedford, but Arthur, Warwick, and Percy entered Bedford Modern School in January, 1885. Samuel and his wife lived at Le Chalet, Geary Street in Bedford until the family returned to Devon to live in Exmouth in about 1889. Fanny, escorted by Herbert, went to New Zealand to marry her cousin John Bullied, who owned a large drapery business in Oamaru in which Herbert was for some years in partnership with his brother-in-law. Ernest was admitted as a solicitor of the English Supreme Court in 1885 and went to New Zealand in 1886, where he qualified as a barrister as well as a solicitor. His parliamentary career did not begin until 1911. Edgar was made deacon at Oxford in 1885 and became curate of Chipping Norton. Kathleen probably went with her father, stepmother, and the younger children to Derby but nothing is known of her at this time except that she was beginning to think about becoming a nun. It was not until December, 1886 that she entered the Anglican Convent of the Society of St. Margaret, East Grinstead, as a postulant, a few weeks before Leah's marriage.

We may now turn to the movements of Leah, which are only partly known. However, a few details may be added to what has already been published. Having completed her schooling at Exeter she went to a boarding school in Switzerland, where she learned French and German. She was at home when her mother died, but when the ex-governess took over the running of the household she went back again to Switzerland, and thence to Berlin. At the time of writing, a daughter of Herbert Lee, Mrs. Harwood, tells me that her father was quite definite in stating that Leah went to Berlin to become some sort of governess to the Empress Augusta's children. He added that the large Empress, remarking Leah's slimness, as later did Jules, used to call her "my dear little Leah." Apparently Leah was recommended to the post by the principal of the school in Switzerland. It would seem that this appointment did not last and was over by the time Jules came to her for the English pronunciation lessons in January, 1886. He may well have known her before this time. Jules relates in his letter of September 8, 1886 that by that time Leah had been in Berlin for two years, living partly on an allowance from her father and partly on what she earned from her lessons. He does not mention her employment with the Empress, but he has already shown that he muddled the occupations of the brothers and in this letter he says that Leah's mother had died four years previously, when it was almost exactly three years. May he not have been so in love that he forgot to mention her employment with the Empress? He may have had reasons for not telling that he knew her at this time. At any rate, by January 1886 Leah was employed by no one and was free to study painting and to spend time painting when she was not giving English lessons.

The story of the courtship and marriage is already well known. The wedding present of the Louis XV tea set was given not only to Jules but to Leah also, and in addition the Empress gave her two dresses for her "little sisters," one of which was later given to Herbert Lee's daughter but was unhappily not preserved. Leah's engagement ring is, however, in the same lady's safekeeping.

Leah was by no means out of touch with her family during her short married life. When Jules died on August 20, 1887 a telegram was immediately sent to her sister Kathleen at the Convent at East Grinstead and she left for Paris on the same day, returning after the funeral on August 24. She later told her family that she thought the funeral was conducted in a very perfunctory and callous manner.

After her husband's death Leah visited England at some time. Her father sent her to Menton in December 1887 for the sake of her health, but there was no improvement. She returned and entered St. Peter's Home, Kilburn, where she died in June, 1888. Her brother Edgar travelled from the Isle of Skye, where he was then priest in charge of a mission, to conduct the funeral service at Teignmouth in Devon, where Leah had lived as a child.

Little more can be said about Leah's sad life after the death of Jules, except that a few days before her death she talked of her meeting with Jules as the happiest event of her life, although before their marriage Jules had doubted that he could ever make any woman happy.

Laforgue and Baudelaire

Raymond Poggenburg

Comparisons do not have to be odious, but may just as easily be compliments. Any poet knows that. Thus a linking of Laforgue's name with Baudelaire's should suggest his importance without leading us to make the kind of critical comparison unfair to a poet who died at twenty-seven, long before fully realizing his great promise.

I should like to propose that the poetic task Laforgue set himself was no less ambitious than the one Baudelaire had accomplished. That task, the essential act of self-identification through artistic creation, Baudelaire brought to fulfillment when he wrote *Les Fleurs du mal*. It would be unreasonable to say that Laforgue's work shows a comparable achievement but his direction is unmistakable. He, too, wished to become a *poète absolu*, to use the phrase invented by Verlaine.

Published in 1857, three years before Laforgue's birth, *Les Fleurs du mal* was to become not only a model but a force in itself, a challenge and an example to later poets. Its powerfully ordered construction, its dense richness of imagery, its profoundly human lyricism all combine to make of it the most influential single poetic statement of our time.

The reason for this position of eminence lies, I think, in the challenge Baudelaire accepted in writing those poems and in his composing them into a whole that finally can be accepted as an utterly complete lyrical expression of himself. I should take Verlaine's phrase to mean that nothing interfered between poet and poetry, that no occasion dictated poetic creation, that the poet showed as much honesty in its writing as his art would permit. The important thing about *Les Fleurs du mal* is not that they portray evil; it is more remarkable that they give us Baudelaire, a very great artist, showing us this world seen by his subtle self. That achievement is a view of the world as it is, and of himself as he is, expressed in a style entirely personal and therefore new, the work of an uncompromising artist. Neither unchecked lyric outpouring nor formalistic excess mar the even tone of the verse, regardless of its subject. Total control of entire intensity marks that masterful performance.

Les Fleurs du mal, or more properly speaking, the poetic authority and identity of Baudelaire, opened the way for the great Symbolists: Mallarmé, Rimbaud, Verlaine. After an early Baudelairean phase, clearly visible in his first verse, Mallarmé chose or was impelled into a path which led him eventually to memorialize chance in *Un Coup de dés jamais n'abolira le hasard*. Rimbaud, less rarefied, in his youthful voyage into *voyance*, with its disillusioned return to reality, looked on Baudelaire as a *"vrai Dieu."* Verlaine's lyrical recreation of a uniquely poetic existence can be best understood and admired when we see him as one of a line extending back through Baudelaire to François Villon. All three gave different answers to the challenge laid down by *Les Fleurs du mal*, and have taken their places with Baudelaire in the small company of those whose works have not diminished in vitality because they have gone

Au fond de l'Inconnu pour trouver du nouveau!

I should like now to point to evidence for my belief that Laforgue heard that challenge clearly, and that his answer had much of the authority one senses in the work of the three major poets of his time. The authority rests on his authentic individuality, distinguishable from those of the other three men and springing from a vision profoundly like that of Baudelaire.

Whatever the differences between them, the Man of *Les Fleurs du mal* was still in all important ways the Man Laforgue sought in himself. He was an artist first of all but intensely aware of the genius of his time, which was less the slave of Beauty than of Progress. He was aware of the deep chasm separating his world from the average person's, and felt his own isolation. Even though possessed of a deeply-felt religious sense he did not find solace in organized worship. Before making good his commitment to Art, Laforgue had to discover himself as a man and as an artist, and it is this search that makes his verse so moving.

Laforgue was unlike Mallarmé, whose jewel-like structures bear little resemblance to these almost casually graceful poems. Rimbaldian ebullience finds no echo in him (although he calls that young redskin genius *la seule isomère de Baudelaire*). Verlaine's lack of decorum is totally foreign to Laforgue's poetic style.

Laforgue's poetry depends for its beauty neither on formal complication, nor on sheer power nor on lyrical directness. It strikes rather a special chord, one we continue to hear in our daily lives, a chord arising from our common experiences in conflict with our uncommon longings, as we suspect that our lives are no more meaningful than a popular song or that Bach's magnificent organ music may be glorifying mere emptiness. Laforgue's pitch is on a human level and Ennui, the Baudelairean *monstre délicat*, is not to be evaded but to be conquered by human means. It is for this approach to Beauty that we must respect him, for it may well be the hardest of all the challenges implicit in Baudelaire's heritage. Laforgue might have attempted escape; his poetic gifts were such that he could have taken refuge in esthetic dilettantism, turning his hand to less demanding problems than self-discovery. Instead, isolated in the Pascalian position, Laforgue looked inward with an uncompromising gaze and outward with a discerning eye. Ironically alert to the implications of modernity, he went about developing a poetic style proper to himself and to his age. Gone at twenty-seven, the younger man hardly had time to establish his position in the world of French letters. In addition, his five years away from that world as a reader to the Empress Augusta of Saxe-Weimar took him far from the scene of the experiences that made Baudelaire so Parisian a poet. Unlike Baudelaire, Laforgue married, and even if one were to consider Jeanne Duval Baudelaire's wife (as he often referred to his mistress), it is enough to compare Jeanne with Leah Lee to see the temperamental differences between the two men. The *Vénus Noire* and the *petit personnage* have less in common than any two women one could imagine, I believe. Although Laforgue acquired, on his return from Germany, first-hand knowledge of the difficult life of the man of letters in Paris, he did not have to endure the grinding consequences, prolonged over many years, of debts incurred during a thoughtless youth. Nor did he develop the bitterness of the older man, whose condition was made even less bearable by the knowledge that his mother, had she wished to do so, could have cleared away his indebtedness, leaving him without any fortune but free of a paralysing situation. In short, there are few reasons, if any, to seek biographical grounds for comparison between the two men.

Their poetry is frequently as dissimilar as their lives. It is impossible to imagine Baudelaire writing a poem such as "Complainte des pianos qu'on entend dans les quartiers aisés," with its beautiful evocation of the sensations aroused in the poet who hears the sounds of the scales played obediently by young girls as they await their "composers" like sad, well-bred sirens on the gray rocks of the Faubourg Saint-Germain. And when Laforgue tries his hand at a Baudelairean theme the results are hardly pleasing. To choose an example at random, "La Première Nuit" is more like a pastiche than an original composition:

> Voici venir le Soir, doux au vieillard lubrique.
> Mon chat Mürr accroupi comme un sphinx héraldique
> Contemple, inquiet, de sa prunelle fantastique
> Marcher à l'horizon la lune chlorotique.
>
> C'est l'heure où l'enfant prie, où Paris-lupanar
> Jette sur le pavé de chaque boulevard
> Ses filles aux seins froids qui, sous le gaz blafard
> Voguent, flairant de l'oeil un mâle de hasard.
>
> Mais près de mon chat Mürr, je rêve à ma fenêtre.
> Je songe aux enfants qui partout viennent de naître.
> Je songe à tous les morts enterrés d'aujourd'hui.
>
> Et je me figure être au fond du cimetière,
> Et me mets à la place, en entrant dans leur bière,
> De ceux qui vont passer là leur première nuit.

The first five lines resound with echoes of no fewer than twelve of Baudelaire's poems and the idea is something to the effect that while people die, others are born at the same moment, rather a weak mainspring for a form as demanding as the sonnet. Despite all the Baudelairean paraphernalia (the Poet, the cat, the *filles*, the cemetery) the poem lacks any real substance and its tone is layered on, however skillfully. Its effect does not proceed from any vital center, as is the case with Baudelaire's poems.

Included in Laforgue's unpublished verse are several other imitative efforts ("Guitare," "Excuse macabre," "La Complainte des montres"). All show a lack of mastery that Laforgue himself doubtless recognized and nowhere does one hear an accent wholly Baudelairean or, for that matter, quite Laforguian.

Laforgue's idea of Baudelaire, to judge from the "Notes sur Baudelaire" he left behind, did not take fully into account the older poet's achievement. In fact, it almost seems on reading these briefly sketched impressions that Laforgue did not really wish to draw close to Baudelaire's real identity, that he was trying to escape the pull of *Les Fleurs du mal*. It is curious to see how Verlaine refers to Baudelaire (Je ne t'ai pas connu, je ne t'ai pas aimé . . .) and to think that Mallarmé was obliged, as he said, to "debaudelairize" himself. When Laforgue says of Baudelaire, "Les angoisses métaphysiques ne sont pas pour le toucher, l'épiderme de son âme est d'un autre tissu" we wonder what he must have thought of poems such as "Châtiment de l'orgueil," "La Destruction," "Les Litanies de Satan," "L'Examen de Minuit," "Le Rebelle" et "L'Imprévu." While these indicate Baudelaire's sensitivity to other than physical anguish, one must look for the totality of his feelings in *Les Fleurs du mal* taken as a whole. Nowhere did he attempt to systematize his views. He did show great interest in such systems, so much is clear from his involvement with De Maistre and with Poe. The latter's "Eureka," translated by Baudelaire, seemed to present a rationalized theory of the universe, unifying the material and the spiritual. It may also be true that the idea of the metaphysical often leads to that of the theological; even so, Baudelaire never chose that path. Whatever his relationship with his God may have been, it was a personal one. Laforgue, perhaps during his long period of reading at the Bibliothèque Nationale, envisioned a somewhat more grandiose approach. A book of verse, a book of tales, and a volume of prophecy were to compose his works. The last of these was to provoke an apocalyptic scene in which the earth in mourning leaves a train of lamentations as it spins on through space. It all reminds one of the Œuvre of which Mallarmé dreamed, of the seer's truth Rimbaud sought. Perhaps Laforgue's ironical position called for some sort of systematic bridge back to effective action. Perhaps he felt a need for an abstract, philosophical substitute for religion; but one cannot help wondering whether, with his extraordinary poetic gift, he truly needed such an aid. It seems to me that he had not yet really understood the essential, creative role of the poet, different from that of the scholar or philosopher. What Baudelaire seemed to know is that Poetry discovers itself, and therefore Beauty. It is neither Philosophy nor Religion. Laforgue appears occasionally to be trying to find an order that will make life amenable to art, while Baudelaire rather insists upon making order of his life through his art. In this connection, it would be interesting to know just what Laforgue thought of Edgar Allan Poe, whose views on controlled composition show a commitment to the ideal of system in art which, to be valid, must correspond to a larger notion of a universal systematic order, or to Nature in the largest sense of the word. Baudelaire was careful, though, to distinguish Poe's quality of imagination as most useful in the *nouvelle*, remarking that it did not suffice for the creation of the most priceless literary treasure: Poetry. Poe's kind of imagination, he suggests, the conscious perception of relationships among things, of correspondence in a nonpoetic sense, is the property of system-maker, of philosopher, of theologian. The *Derniers Vers,* however, seem to offer indications that Laforgue's lyric gift was asserting itself and that his verse would soon be in need of no props. Many confident notes are struck and, what is perhaps more significant, struck repeatedly, for he was going back over his earlier verse, choosing the most viable parts, moving towards the self-affirmation that marks the successful lyric poet.

For Laforgue, myth and legend did not offer the possibilities they seem to have for many moderns. He used it in the lightest of manners, giving the *Moralités légendaires* an offhand, mocking tone having little in common with Baudelaire's almost reverent application of the looming figures of Sisyphus, Andromache, and many others. Less tortured by the Present than Laforgue, Baudelaire was able to use legend and myth to help establish the continuum of man's artistic creation, the continuum of "Les Phares."

In some ways, Laforgue's esthetics seems to have been an outgrowth of Baudelaire's, seeking beauty in the commonplace, admitting words and ideas that would have been rejected by traditional standards. Not content with this, Laforgue uses puns and neologisms, avoiding any externally imposed canon of language, making his poetry depend for its dignity upon the inherently admirable character of the poet. Although it is true that Baudelaire often uses terms that Racine might have avoided, no great linguistic shock, so to speak, is produced by *Les Fleurs du mal.* Rather, one is impressed by a general sobriety of language dealing with subjects that under ordinary circumstances might have called forth a different response. Moreover, Baudelaire's poetry has a classical firmness of meter and rhyme, while Laforgue's less consciously constructed lines seem always to be seeking their own form.

Baudelairean irony is always accompanied, as he says, by what he calls *le surnaturel*. It does not have the same kind of detachment one feels in Laforgue's verse. Richly endowing *Les Fleurs du mal* is an atmosphere one may call mystical, or simply accept as the kind of intensity generated by the emotional force of the poetry. Laforgue, in "Autre Complainte de Lord Pierrot," clearly displays the source of his own ironical attitude. The fundamental dialogue between affective and nonaffective in Pierrot ends in the serio-comic stance in which love is made impossible by mathematics, faith is destroyed by skepticism, and communication is blocked by paradox. The result is a highly intellectualized irony that leaves the poet wondering why he is alive. When no reassurance is forthcoming, certain teleological questions arise, involving the great ideas of Evil, of Nature, of Death. These were the questions to which Laforgue was addressing himself when he died, the questions Baudelaire had answered out of the center of himself in *Les Fleurs du mal*. Nature, for Baudelaire, was in large measure the source of Evil; Death was, in Wallace Stevens' words, the Mother of Beauty. For Laforgue at the end of his short life, Nature was surely the force to be reckoned with but not yet to be cursed. In a short poem filled with echoes of Ronsard and Malherbe, coming last in the series called *Des Fleurs de bonne volonté* (obviously a Baudelairean reference) Laforgue makes clear his position. "Air de Biniou" simply states his faith that poetry is valuable but that it cannot have the limitless expansion it would need to be able to express All. Nature, he says, provides joy only as long as we do not cease to woo her, for when we stop seeking life she will kill us. Let Nature do as she will, let everything be as she commands, we shall cultivate the Nine Muses (he calls them the Immortal Gleaners) in the hope that we may escape the hold Nature has over us. In this poem one hears no echoes of Baudelairean *Correspondances*. The classical tone of the poem has little *expansion des choses infinies* and none of the magisterial sweep of "Les Phares." Faced by the spectacle of Nature with its all but impossible challenge to the poet, Laforgue elects the Baudelairean solution: artistic creation in the face of every difficulty. The theme of the poem is a major one, its execution clearly in a minor mode.

In *Derniers Vers* Laforgue takes firmer hold of the central problem. "L'Hiver qui vient," the first poem, comes as a revelation of what Laforgue has been attempting. The pun, "Blocus sentimental!" is boldly raised to the intensity Laforgue seeks, setting the poem free and moving as would the opening bars of a Schönberg piece, where all the notes of the twelve-tone scale are heard. He reduces to these symbolic terms all the intense personal emotion scattered through the poetry, placing them in right setting.

The poems now begin to show greater integrity. For example, "Dimanches" ("Bref, j'allais me donner d'un 'Je vous aime'. . . .") incorporates a number of the poet's major concerns: Anomia ("Mon Moi, c'est Galathée aveuglant Pygmalion . . ."); Isolation ("Vae Soli! . . ."); the Young Girl (". . . à l'ivoirin paroissien . . ."); the Piano, opposed now to the Walkyries; and finally a new note, that of Suicide ("Va donc acheter deux sous d'ellébore . . ."), comes to close the poem. There is a greater degree of density; thought and expression are quite economical in spite of the technical freedom.

Another poem entitled "Dimanches" ("C'est

l'automne, l'automne, l'automne . . .") unites the themes of Love, Analysis, Nature, the Ideal, Death. It suggests a deep yearning for fulfillment and dramatically illustrates Laforgue's insistence upon the human dimension this must have. "Pétition," a poem that hovers on the verge of the didactic, puts into general terms Laforgue's ideas on women, which closely resemble one side of Baudelaire's attitude in the famous lines:

> Mon enfant, ma soeur,
> songe à la douceur
> D'aller là-bas vivre ensemble . . .

Woman should be, according to Laforgue, a sister and an equal, not the eternal adversary of Baudelaire's "Duellum."

"Simple Agonie" sounds another new note: that of Destruction. It came for Laforgue when he was just the age of Baudelaire at the time the latter describes in his *Journaux intimes*, that of the Revolution of 1848. Almost wonderingly, Baudelaire refers to his taste for destruction in May of that year. He attributes this desire to the natural in himself. Laforgue, on the other hand, sees the only solution to the world's ills in a general destruction and then, presumably, in a rebuilding. The introduction of this idea comes as a surprise, since Laforgue has hardly shown any tendency to change his introspective, almost elegiac, tone up to this point. One wonders if he was correct in calling Rimbaud *la seule isomère de Baudelaire*. It is hard not to remember the words Rimbaud spoke before the Louvre: "On aurait dû brûler tout cela."

"Solo de lune" brings out yet another development. For the first time Laforgue seems to be writing about two people in one of his descriptions of an *amour manqué*, not only about himself. The usual theme of sadness at not having been able to fall in love is strengthened by a note of real concern for the partner, not only as lover but also as a sister, in keeping with Laforgue's ideal. I think this is a sign of maturation; content is growing beneath form. "Oh! qu'une, d'Elle-même, un beau soir, sût venir" puts the sentimental drama of Laforgue into verse increasingly firmer and less boyish. It becomes clear that Laforgue has become conscious of one of his major means of poetic dynamism, the achievement of significant existence through love of Woman.

The concluding strophe of the last poem in *Derniers Vers* contains an apparently direct allusion to one of Baudelaire's major poems, "Un Voyage à Cythère." Laforgue addresses a young woman, his sweetheart, and, as is his custom, carries on an ironical dialogue with himself at the same time. The subject of the poem is the poet's desire to find emotional fulfillment in the face of life's monotony, to find love in spite of his critical hesitancy.

> *Eh bien, pour aimer ce qu'il y a d'histoires*
> *Derrière ces beaux yeux d'orpheline héroïne,*
> *O Nature, donne-moi la force et le courage*
> *De me croire en âge,*
> *O Nature, relève-moi le front!*
> *Puisque, tôt ou tard, nous mourrons . . .*
> ("*Noire bise, averse glapissante*")

As the passage indicates, he turns not to a deity but to a generalized idea, Nature. The major themes of Innocence, Love, Death, and Nature are woven into a Laforguian background of urban ugliness under a hostile sky, the décor of exile, against which stands the poet.

In Baudelaire's "Un Voyage à Cythère," the concluding lines run:

> *Dans ton île, ô Vénus! je n'ai trouvé debout*
> *Qu'un gibet symbolique où pendait mon image . . .*
> *—Ah! Seigneur! donnez-moi la force et le courage*
> *De contempler mon coeur et mon corps sans dégoût!*

The Baudelaire poem is an allegorical journey to the island of Love, with an unhappy discovery as its reward. Laforgue still awaits his own departure. Baudelaire calls upon his God to give him the strength to continue living, after the knowledge that Love will not redeem him. Laforgue calls upon Nature to help him love in the face of Death.

In spite of their deep differences, Laforgue and Baudelaire are linked by certain profoundly shared concerns. The most important of these is probably the desire to achieve modernity. After Baudelaire, Laforgue continued the search for the genius of the contemporary. His material, like Baudelaire's, was uncompromisingly drawn from the world that met his senses and his shaping imagination never sought escape into dream or fancy. Both men proceed from a deeply perceived realization of what has come best to be defined in a Baudelairean word: *le Mal*. Whether understood metaphysically or socially, the force of Evil in the world is for both men an active, powerful agent. Laforgue sees it as omnipotent and omnipresent, Good as accidental and transitory. Baudelaire makes of it the central truth of human conduct, the destiny of Man and around it constructs the extraordinarily compelling complex of poems that compose *Les Fleurs du mal*. In Laforgue, however, there is always a movement towards a more optimistic possibility, no matter how tentative it may be (the partitive in *Des Fleurs de bonne volonté* is an indication). All the reverberations of Baudelaire's verse come, finally, from the singleness of the note struck; he forces us, almost brutally, to attend to his vision. Laforgue's world, although far from sunny, is not yet the world of concentrated Evil in which Baudelaire's lines live, but whatever his view of it, it was still most Baudelairean in character.

Laforgue Among the Symbolists

Henri Peyre

There is probably no more singular phenomenon in the whole range of the comparative history of European literatures than the extraordinary prestige and influence of French Symbolism outside France. Neither the *Pléiade* nor the writers of the seventeenth century whom the French subsequently consecrated as their classics, neither, certainly, the romantics nor even the surrealists and the existentialists enjoyed a comparable success. Only the *Philosophes* of the Age of Enlightenment have exercised in Europe, in South and North America dynamic action of equal importance; but the impact of those prophets of a liberal world is less surprising. Their work concerned the immediate improvement of men's fate and set political passions in play. The role played in Russia, in Germany, in Latin America by Baudelaire, Verlaine, Rimbaud, Mallarmé, Laforgue, and other poets, then (1865–95) read by very few in their own country, affected not only poets and theorists of poetry, but dramatists, novelists, painters and musicians, generations of students who later became statesmen, men of affairs, diplomats, ambulance drivers who urged young Americans to enlist in the army and fight on French soil because France was the land of poetry. F. S. Flint wrote as much while the United States was still undecided about entering the first World War.

On the eve of that war, William Butler Yeats, attending a banquet arranged in his honor by the editors of *Poetry: A Magazine of Verse* in Chicago, upbraided American poets for persevering in all that he and other Europeans had rebelled against some years earlier: "the sentimentality, the rhetoric, the 'moral uplift.'" He pointed out the reason for such a lag: "not because you are too far from England, but because you are too far from France. It is from Paris that nearly all the great influences in art and literature have come, from the time of Chaucer until now. Today, the metrical experiments of the French poets are overwhelming us by their variety and delicacy." [1]

Yeats' overly generous tribute to those ancient or foreign writers to whom he thought he was indebted, "the builders of his soul," as he called the classics, was as exaggerated as Gide's. Like all so-called influences, this one was in truth the realization of a latent need formulated and fulfilled by others. Poets of several nations sensed that the French had, with more revolutionary energy than was theirs, turned against what was effete, lax, and declamatory in the romantics and advocated a return to the hard, concise, lucidly outlined poetry which Pound and many South American poets admired in Théophile Gautier, subsequently in Rimbaud. The Anglo-Americans may also have been impressed, perhaps to an excess, by the ease with which the French evolve theories to support their poetic practice. Since the Italian sonneteers and humanists, none have taken questions of language and poetic technique quite as seriously; few critics outside Paris have deemed it their function to fight such furious wars of words around literary works. The originality of the poets of England and America remained intact, however, as did that of the poets of Russia, of Germany, of Spain after 1898. Mallarmé helped Joyce

to become himself as Valéry helped the greatest of
them all, Rilke, and Laforgue aided in the revelation
of the essential Eliot. In the case of the last two, it was
the function of the French to assist in the poetic
growth of authors more profound than themselves.
Such has occasionally been the fate of teachers and
innovators.

Laforgue's compatriots have, meanwhile, been more
than a little puzzled by the warmth of the tribute paid
to him in the English-speaking countries, and this
applies even to those French readers who have long
professed to admire and enjoy his best verse—certain
of the *Complaintes* and his last poems. Few would go
so far as those Americans who have smiled condescend-
ingly at the Frenchification of Edgar Allan Poe or as
Aldous Huxley when he singled out the American
revered by such expert judges as Baudelaire, Mallarmé,
and Valéry as the paragon of "vulgarity in literature."
What is vulgar in Laforgue stems from his youth and
his poses; and he is untainted by the morbidity of
Poe's obsession with love and death indissolubly wed-
ded. Nevertheless French readers are even more dis-
concerted than they are flattered to find T. S. Eliot,
no doubt the most influential critic of our age, declar-
ing (in 1928, introducing Pound's *Selected Poems*)
that "the form in which [he] began to write, in 1908
or 1909, was directly drawn from the study of Laforgue
together with the later Elizabethans"! Elsewhere, in
the *Criterion* of January 1930, Eliot added that Laforgue spoke to his generation "more intimately than
Baudelaire seemed to do." He drew a parallel between
John Donne and Laforgue (and Corbière): in all
three, "the pattern is given by what goes on within the
mind, rather than by the exterior events which provoke the mental activity and play of thought and
feeling." Later still, in 1934, in the second edition of

his *Selected Essays*, Eliot, still ranking Laforgue with Donne and with Baudelaire, hailed him as "the inventor of an attitude, a system of feeling or of morals."

The explanation for the difference of attitudes between Laforgue's readers from both sides of the Atlantic, or of the Channel, did not escape Eliot's lucid mind. A foreign reader often feels drawn to an author relatively new and unknown to those around him, not yet praised by teachers or schoolmates. Laforgue, discovered through Arthur Symons, was, around 1908–10, unknown to Eliot's friends, even in the most sophisticated circles of Harvard. Eliot, moreover, wanted to write poetry and he was aware of the need for a thorough renovation of technique after Rossetti, Swinburne, Hardy, and the Georgians. Gerard Manley Hopkins was then unknown and unpublished. Rimbaud was too enigmatic and impossible to imitate in another language or in his own. Verlaine's music could not be matched in another idiom and his sensibility had nothing in common with that of the austere young man from Missouri. He turned to Laforgue for models of a free verse safer for a beginner to imitate if it was expertly written in another language than his own; he further found in Laforgue the dissociation of sensibility, the bitter humor which he was looking for in the late Elizabethans and in the English Metaphysicals. Such an influence, coming from abroad and exercised by a poet dead for at least twenty years, offered no risk. It was not even to be perceived, still less denounced, by the reviewers of "The Love Song of J. Alfred Prufrock," Eliot's most "Laforguian poem" or by readers of *The Waste Land* in 1923. The latter was sanctimoniously criticized in the *Times Literary Supplement* of September 20, 1923, for its author's "disinclination to awake in us a direct emotional response" and its acrobatics while "walking very near the limits of coherence." In an article on the poetry of Yeats published in *Purpose* in 1940, Eliot put the case cogently, both as he had experienced it and as future generations might profit from that example:

"A very young man, who is himself stirred to write . . . is looking for masters who will elicit his consciousness of what he wants to say himself, of the kind of poetry that is in him to write. The taste of an adolescent writer is intense but narrow, is determined by personal needs. The kind of poetry that I needed, to teach me the use of my own voice, did not exist in English at all; it was only to be found in French." [2]

Why has Laforgue seemed less original to the French than to such keen appraisers of poetry as those American architects of the modernist movement in English? Even the academic critics for whom the technique, the ideas, the sensibility of Laforgue should have offered an opportunity for university courses of relative originality, and a varied supply of thesis topics, have been strangely silent. Mme Durry, in her long, well-informed, sensitive introduction to the Laforgue volume in the "Poètes d'aujourd'hui" series and Pierre Reboul, in a condensed presentation of the man and his works in another collection, "Connaissance des lettres," are the only exceptions among the French professors, and their volumes appeared only after 1950, more than two-thirds of a century after Laforgue's death. Guy Michaud, in his *Message poétique du Symbolisme,* in 1947, treated Laforgue with more generosity and more perceptiveness than other historians of the Symbolist movement, who, overimpressed by the label "decadent," had often chosen to grant him only niggardly space, as if he had been waylaid in one of the minor byways of French poetry.

It is customary, and not a little cruel, for the French to dismiss Laforgue's verse as marked with "emotional immaturity." Youthful enthusiasm for his more eccentric poems, evinced by Alain-Fournier and Jacques Rivière, when students of twenty in a Paris *lycée*, was soon followed by more critical scrutiny: the two young men, in their haste to devour the works of their predecessors, found themselves successively in Henri de Régnier's gentle *odelettes*, in Laforgue's sarcastic *complaintes*, then in Claudel, then in Gide. Harsher than his more imaginative and dreamy friend whose constant thought was the elaboration of the novel of his youth transfigured, *Le Grand Meaulnes*, Rivière soon came to list his reasons for detaching himself from Laforgue: they were the sort of reasons which a young man, anxious to outgrow the naïve enthusiasms of his adolescence, discovers for himself when he becomes ashamed of his recent immaturity. Rivière found fault, in a severe letter of April 23, 1906, with Laforgue's technical virtuosity and mastery over verbal pyrotechnics, with his egocentric concern with himself and the eternal misunderstanding between man and woman. He even added "a blasphemy: what a happiness for him to have died so young!", suspecting that Laforgue's capacity for self-renewal was very low indeed. The slur is grossly unfair. No other poet of the second Symbolist generation, neither Régnier nor Moréas, neither Samain nor Vielé-Griffin, showed, at twenty-seven, an equal ability to pass from one source of inspiration to another and to take himself mercilessly to task. One is reminded, reading the posthumous essays and the correspondence of Laforgue (much of it unavailable to Fournier and Rivière in 1905–06), of none other than John Keats. A careful study of the evolution of his mind and of his sensibility, as well as of his workmanship as both a poet and a prose writer second only to Mallarmé in the latter capacity among the writers of those years, has never been undertaken, while his friend Gustave Kahn has been honored by a huge monograph written in French by an English professor, John C. Ireson. The timidity of French scholars is in this case inexplicable.

So is their reluctance to write searchingly on irony, a word and notion which they have relinquished to German critics, from the Schlegels, Jean Paul and Tieck to Thomas Mann. Friedrich Schlegel, in a curious passage in *Lyceumsfragment* 108, defined irony as "a feeling of the irreconcilable conflict of the absolute and the relative, of the impossibility and necessity of complete communication. It is the freest of all licences, for it enables us to rise above ourselves." He identifies irony, indistinguishable from humor in his view, as the original feature of romanticism. Ever since the romantics, indeed, irony has served to convey the contrast between the author's assertion of his awareness of his own freedom and his realization that he cannot reach the infinite of his dreams; his creation remains finite and paltry, and the creator can only look at it with mockery. That irony, with perhaps a sharper, more Voltairean intellectual note, is as present in French romanticism as it is in German: in Musset, in Nerval, and also in Hugo, in Gautier, and Baudelaire, and certainly in Mallarmé's extraordinary prose poems and in the letters of his early manhood. Laforgue is the virtuoso of that "equilibrium of opposed impulses," as I. A. Richards called it. At times his affectation of insolence is a trifle disconcerting.

> "... *en attendant la mort,*
> *Je fume au nez des dieux de fines cigarettes.*"

There was a little of the clown in him, and he played his part in imposing the clown-figure on French poets and painters as their symbol. Apollinaire, and among the surrealists, Desnos and Péret, and the poets occasionally termed "Cubists" (Cendrars, Cocteau, Jacob, the latter ungrateful in his mentions of Laforgue) are successors to the poet of the *Complaintes* and of *L'Imitation de Notre-Dame la Lune.* Ironical, witty, entertaining verse, barely accepted by scholars in the case of Villon, has, when written by the *Rhétoriqueurs* who were nearly *grands*, by the seventeenth-century *libertins*, by Voltaire, Musset, Hugo, been unfairly banished from anthologies of French poetry, to the advantage of both sentimental and philosophical genres.

Not that the last two were lacking in Laforgue, one of the few complete poets of his age! If the people of France (the country which Baudelaire claimed he was gladly leaving for Brussels, because everyone in France resembled Voltaire) appear reluctant to admit that irony can coexist with poetry, and even enhance it, they who can be outrageously sentimental in life and on the screen are averse to admitting sentimentality in literature. The aging, hardening process leads men still comparatively young to dismiss rather scornfully both *Sans Famille* and *Le Petit Chose*, the mystical yearnings of days of catechism, and the sentimental outpourings of Lamartine and Verlaine. Young Englishmen likewise sneer at *Enoch Arden*, at "The Charge of the Light Brigade"; young Americans at Longfellow. Werther's letters preceding his suicide, or *Hermann und Dorothea*, enjoy a similar reception from young Germans of today. One might speculate on the divorce between literature and life which prevents the expression of powerful emotions, such as the death of a child or mother or the striving for the persistence of mutual love in married life, in poetry or in fiction—Dickens and Tolstoy notwithstanding.

Recourse to glib phrases like "artistic restraint" and "aesthetic distance," or the suggestive power of understatement, has never provided an adequate explanation. The sentimental strain in Laforgue seldom descends to the vulgar tone Parisians adore in their songs plaintively mouthed by popular singers but dislike in literature destined for an élite. It springs from as true an anguish at the absurdity of man's fate in a universe to which he is not attuned as Kafka, Camus, or Beckett may have experienced and expressed in our day. As in the case of these later writers, the emotion is deftly relieved by a wry smile and a rare felicitousness of phrasing. Laforgue might have confessed, with Corbière:

"Mon coeur fait de l'esprit—le sot—pour se leurrer."

Laforgue is close enough to the popular poetry of his countrymen to remain, for all his sophistication and apparent egotism, a man of the people. Almost alone among the Symbolists of 1880–95, he learned to shun idealistic flights into the empyrean and visions of disembodied Beatrices. We know too little about his literary tastes and he was probably, during his five years at the German court, too scantily informed about literary developments in Paris for us to be sure that he appreciated Zola, as Mallarmé did. We may, however, bearing in mind André Breton's contention that the true poetry of that age is to be found in the Naturalists rather than in the self-conscious and ethereal Symbolists, praise Laforgue for having heeded the common life of the French capital and the everyday speech of ordinary men. He attempted to write a new kind of poetry drawn directly from the prosaic and from that daily life which he found deplorably "quotidienne." "Make a work which is alive and the rest will take care of itself" was one of the counsels he offered,

at a time when Gide (a few years before the very
Laforguian *Paludes*) and his young friends were intox-
icated with hothouse literature.

Philosophical poetry has not enjoyed the favor of
critics in our century. True, a number of notorious
failures incurred by men of ideas endeavoring to be
poets (Sully-Prudhomme and Guyau among Laforgue's contemporaries, J. A. Symonds and George
Santayana in English) have lent credence to Mallarmé's too often quoted remark that poetry is made
with words, not with ideas. Yet Mallarmé himself was
a poet who thought deeply. Such were Lucretius, and
Goethe, and Shelley, and Baudelaire. Such were Leconte de Lisle—and Laforgue.

T. S. Eliot, in one of his best known essays, "The
Use of Poetry and the Use of Criticism," submitted as
evident that "for a poet to be a philosopher, he would
have to be virtually two men." He added that nothing
could be gained by such schizophrenia. "The work is
better performed inside two skulls than one." Eliot,
while he thought deeply on literary matters, displayed
in fact no special profundity in his overpraised pro-
nouncements on Dante or on culture, and his youthful dissertation on F. H. Bradley should never have
been published. He was no original philosopher. He
had rightly remarked, with reference to Seneca's stoi-
cism, that "the poet who thinks is merely the poet
who can express the emotional equivalent of
thought;" and this he did accomplish.

So did Laforgue, and that is a claim to our esteem at
a moment, a century and more after his birth, when
for the first time man has proved able to venture into
interstellar space and when philosophy has invaded
much fiction and criticism, if not poetry. Critics cus-
tomarily immolate Laforgue's early poems to his later
ones.

"Les grandes angoisses métaphysiques
Ont passé à l'état de chagrins domestiques,"

he wrote wryly, and perhaps with nostalgic regret. True, Laforgue's bolder experiments with language and metrics came mostly in his *Derniers Vers*, written at twenty-six and -seven and published in 1890, privately, three years after his death.[3] But those which he had, in the early 1880's entitled *Le Sanglot de la Terre* (not published in his lifetime) rank among the few ambitious collections of cosmic and philosophical poetry in French, and they are often successful. Thomas Hardy, A. E. Housman, and even their predecessor in the poetry of "the dreadful night" and of "Weltschmerz," James Thomson, have not risen higher than the French youth who had just lost his Catholic faith, had read astronomy treatises by Camille Flammarion, and substituted a sidereal pessimism for the more self-centered and anthropomorphic melancholy of the romantics. He was closer in those poems to the solemn "Bhagavat" of Leconte de Lisle, or to his evocation of "Les Hurleurs," dogs barking at the moon, and of "le Vent froid de la nuit" (both in *Poèmes barbares*) than to the Symbolists, who seldom aimed at such cosmic heights. But the distinction between the two groups, improperly dubbed "schools," is entirely artificial. Cazalis (otherwise Jean Lahor) was Mallarmé's best friend and a Parnassian after a fashion, like Mallarmé himself when he celebrated Théophile Gautier, like the Henri de Régnier of *Médailles d'argile*. Impassive, Laforgue never was (nor was Leconte de Lisle). The earth which sobs is the objective correlative to which the suffering poet transfers his own passionate anxiety, his "hypertrophic heart" as one of the ballads called it at a time when Laforgue could not have been aware of Rimbaud's "Le Coeur supplicié," more brutal and mournful. The figure of Christ, strangely absent from most nineteenth-century English poetry but omnipresent in French (Lamartine, Vigny, Nerval, Musset, Hugo, Leconte de Lisle, *et al.*), haunts the poet, "a sidereal Christ," no longer the human one. The philosophical reading which Laforgue absorbed (Schopenhauer, and even more, Hartmann) may not, in the view of specialists, be as profound as Hegel or Schelling. Was Epicurus, who inspired the great philosophical poet of antiquity, quite a match for Plato or Aristotle? Laplace and Godwin, who inspired Shelley's early poetry, and Bergson, who may have influenced Proust and Péguy, may not, in posterity's fickle judgments, be deemed as great philosophers as Spinoza, Kant, or Heidegger. The myth of the unconscious, irrational, and identical with life, groping blindly toward consciousness, proved to be a stimulant for the poet's imagination. He saw himself as sailing through submarine depths, amid the archipelagoes of the unconscious, as another French poet also born in Uruguay, Jules Supervielle, was to do in the fine volume of cosmic poetry entitled *Gravitations*.

To have been the master of ironical poetry, with a rich "ironic inheritance" behind him in another literature; to have expressed new nuances of sensibility and attempted to give legitimate sensibility, tempered with intelligence and humor, a modest place in French poetry; to have mounted into interstellar space and vastly enlarged the shrunken domain of literature, so often clinging to the same monotonous themes and fearful of deriving its inspiration from science; to have bequeathed to his successors a new poetic language and an ingeniously mastered free verse; those are Jules Laforgue's claims to count among the significant writers of nineteenth-century France. The French have long been ungrateful to him and are still reticent in exploring his achievements or in working out his innovations toward richer effects. Along with such writers as Laclos, Rétif, Nerval, and, closer to us, Larbaud, Martin du Gard, Romain Rolland, and Apollinaire, Laforgue has been too readily classified as secondary. But the distinction between great and secondary writers is a nefarious one and criteria for so-called "greatness" should be incessantly challenged. French scholars may well be grateful to the American critics who, coming forward where they had proved timid or conventional, have helped restore Laforgue to his rightful place where he, like Shelley's Adonais, "Beacons from the abode where the Eternal are."

Laforgue and His Time

Leo Weinstein

When, in 1891, Jules Huret conducted his interviews on the state of literature,[1] he was surprised to find that the name of Jules Laforgue, some four years after his death, was mentioned eighteen times (and always favorably!), along with those of the best-known figures of the day.[2] Such praise, from authors who hardly knew him and from loyal friends alike, augured well for the future reputation of the poet.

Let us briefly review certain literary landmarks of Laforgue's short lifetime (limiting ourselves to poetry):

1866 The First *Parnasse contemporain*.
1869 Verlaine's *Fêtes galantes*.
1871 The Second *Parnasse contemporain*.
1874 Verlaine's *Romances sans paroles*.
1876 The Third *Parnasse contemporain*.
1876 Mallarmé's *L'Après-midi d'un faune*.
1884 Huysmans' *A Rebours* and Verlaine's *Poètes maudits* reveal Verlaine, Rimbaud, Mallarmé to the uninitiated.
1885 Laforgue's *Complaintes*.
1886 Rimbaud's *Illuminations* are published.
1886 Laforgue's *Imitation de Notre-Dame la Lune*.
1886 Moréas publishes his manifesto of symbolism in *Figaro*.

The 1870's were dominated by materialism in public life and naturalism in literature. Emile Zola was certainly less scientifically inclined than he would give his readers to understand in his theoretical writings, but the general tendency of his work is unfavorable to poetry, because it neglected the mysterious aspects of human existence and of the world around.

After a decade or so of naturalist fare the public was ready for a new, lyrical, imaginative literature. Soon efforts in this direction, mostly from outside France, created a change in intellectual atmosphere.

As early as 1871 the work of an adversary of Auguste Comte had been translated into French: Herbert Spencer, who insists on the notion of the Unknowable. To him the power behind the outward manifestations of the universe is completely impenetrable. Thus Spencer reopened the domains of religion and mystery which positivism and science seemed to have closed for good.

We know the influence that Eduard von Hartmann's *Philosophy of the Unconscious,* translated into French in 1877, had on Laforgue and his contemporaries. Hartmann attacked the bastion of positivism from the psychological vantage point by explaining the world as being governed by an unconscious spirit, all-powerful and subject to no influence.

About 1880 Schopenhauer attains his greatest influence in France. Although not necessarily anti-positivist or anti-scientific, Schopenhauer's pessimism and disavowal of the external world were instrumental in turning the young generation in a more idealistic direction, in giving a more melancholy tone to their writings.

One cannot speak of the period under discussion without mentioning Richard Wagner. Even though *Tannhäuser* had been a failure at the Opéra in 1861, Baudelaire had become a fervent Wagnerian, and by 1879 Pasdeloup had successfully performed Wagner's music in France. When *Lohengrin* was staged in 1887,

Paris had found a new idol. To the poets, Wagner held out a new goal. As early as 1860, in his *Letters on Music*, he had declared that "the most accomplished work of a poet would be, in its final form, a perfect music," and his exhortations and example made some poets think of a literary orchestration of a poem, that is, an effort to accompany a central thread of text with words chosen primarily for their sonorities and evocative qualities.

French music too was moving in a similar direction. The *Société Nationale de Musique*, founded in 1871, counted among its principal supporters César Franck and his students (Vincent d'Indy, Ernest Chausson) along with Camille Saint-Saëns and Gabriel Fauré. The very subject matter chosen by the Franckists for their tone poems indicated the new trend. In 1883, César Franck's *Le Chasseur maudit* and Ernest Chausson's *Viviane* were performed. Henri Duparc selected Bürger's *Lénore*, while d'Indy turned to *Istar* for inspiration.

Finally, the Russian novelists were introduced to French readers by Melchior de Vogüé in 1884. The themes of passion, compassion, and religious fervor had been unfamiliar in the often flatly representational world of naturalist novels. It was as though a hitherto defective heart-valve were being reopened.

No systematic inquiry was needed to show that the last volume of the *Parnasse contemporain* had been the swan song of the Parnassian poets. Leconte de Lisle, to be sure, was still an important figure in the 1880's, but young poets were more likely to turn to the Rue de Rome for advice. Yet Mallarmé, however brilliant his conversation (or monologue) may have been, was not a strong *chef d'école*, as Leconte de Lisle had been, and the young intellectuals therefore soon split into small groups. Mallarmé himself, in his interview with Huret, complains about this situation. "We are witnessing at present," he says, "a spectacle that is truly extraordinary, unique in the entire history of poetry. Every poet is going into his own little corner, playing on his own flute the airs he likes."

As happens frequently when literary enthusiasm is bubbling over without finding an outlet or leadership, small and numerous Bohemian groups were formed. The young enthusiasts, including a great number of dilettantes and others who simply enjoyed the atmosphere of intellectual excitement, protested noisily against their time and society. Their parents and the "older generation" of writers simply did not understand them and the changed conditions. So in protest they dressed quaintly and baptized their clubs with outlandish names: the Hydropathes, the Hirsutes, the Zutistes, the Jemenfoutistes, etc.

These groups were at first less concerned with literature than with political and social problems. A gradual swing toward literature can, however, be detected in their short-lived reviews: *La Nouvelle rive gauche* (1882), *Lutèce* (1883), *La Revue indépendante* (1884) and finally *Le Décadent*, a derisive term which the young Bohemians accepted joyfully. Laforgue himself, who had met Gustave Kahn in 1880 at a meeting of the Hydropathes, uses the term *décadent* as early as 1882 in speaking favorably of the young people in these groups.

Their time, they feel, is different from any previous epoch, and in order to express the subtle nuances and complexity of feelings and physiological sensations, new words, new expressions must be coined. The result is the sort of jargon to be found in a manifesto in *Le Décadent* dated April 10, 1886:

> Nés du surblaséisme d'une civilisation schopenhauéresque, les Décadents ne sont pas une école littéraire. Leur mission n'est pas de fonder. Ils n'ont qu'à détruire, à tomber les vieilleries . . .

Se dissimuler l'état de décadence où nous sommes arrivés serait le comble de l'insenséisme. Religion, moeurs, justice, tout décade ... La société se désagrège sous l'action corrosive d'une civilisation déliquescente. L'homme moderne est un blasé. Affinement d'appétits, de sensations, de goûts, de luxe, de jouissances, névrose, hypnotisme, morphinomanie, charlatanisme scientifique, schopenhauérisme à outrance, tels sont les prodromes de l'évolution sociale.[3]

Soon the flood of neologisms had reached such proportions as to necessitate a glossary where we discover some five hundred new words, among them: abscons, adamantin, albe, attirance, bibliopole, clangorer, emmi, errance, flavescent, fragrance, hiémal, lactescent, lové, marcescent, navrance, radiance, stagnance, torpide, trépider.[4]

Inevitably, the Decadent jargon and the recently published works of Verlaine and Mallarmé opened up rich opportunities for parodies and some of these rank among the best ever produced in France. The most famous collection was entitled: *Les Déliquescences, poèmes décadents d'Adoré Floupette* (1885) by Henri Beauclair and Gabriel Vicaire. Here nobody is spared. First the Decadents:

Nous dont la Fleur dolente est la Rose Trémière,
Nous n'avons plus de coeur, nous n'avons plus de dents!
Pauvres pantins avec un peu de son dedans,
Nous regardons sans voir la ferme et la fermière.

. . . .

Mais, ô Mort du Désir! Inappétence exquise!
Nous gardons le fumet d'une antique Marquise
Dont un Vase de nuit parfume les Dessous!

Verlaine is parodied for his sensuous murmur-poetry:

Je voudrais que mon âme fût
Aussi roide qu'un affût
Aussi remplie qu'un vieux fût. . . .

and for his religious verses:

> *Si tous les huit jours je te paie un cierge,*
> *Ne pourrais-je donc être pardonné?*
> *Je suis un païen, je suis un damné,*
> *Mais je t'aime tant, Canaille de Vierge!*

Finally, Mallarmé gets his share:

> *Amoureuses Hypnotisées*
> *Par l'Indolence des Espoirs,*
> *Ephèbes doux, aux reflets noirs,*
> *Avec des impudeurs rosées.*
>
> *Par le murmure d'un Avé,*
> *Disparus! O miracle Etrange!*
> *Le démon suppléé par l'Ange,*
> *Le vil Hyperbole sauvé!*

Eventually, even the Decadent review *Lutèce* joined in the swelling chorus of parodies;[5] and a poet with as fine a sense of humor as Laforgue could hardly be expected to resist such obvious temptations. In "Complainte de l'automne monotone" we find an unsurpassed parody of Verlaine:

> *Le vent, la pluie, oh! le vent, la pluie!*
> *Antigone, écartez mon rideau;*
>   *Cet ex-ciel tout suie,*
> *Fond-il* decrescendo, statu quo, crescendo?
>   *Le vent qui s'ennuie,*
> *Retourne-t-il bien les parapluies?*

In general, the Decadents have been judged severely both by critics then and now and by poets of the preceding generation.[6] The names of Laurent Tailhade, Ephraïm Mikhaël, Georges Rodenbach are practically forgotten today. Jules Laforgue, quite on the contrary, has not only been spared such sweeping condemnation but his reputation has continued to grow.

The reason Laforgue has survived is, of course, that

he was more than just a Decadent poet—he was also a Symbolist and one of the first in France to employ free verse. But this is merely the exterior aspect of Laforgue. What makes him especially interesting to us is the way he represents a recurring problem: that of a young man with elevated ideals living in a society in which there seems to be no place for him. The same problem had been faced earlier in the nineteenth century by French writers and each one had reacted in his particular manner: Musset, the embodiment of the *mal du siècle* spirit, had plunged into a dissolute life; Stendhal had heaped criticism and ridicule on the Restoration and the July Monarchy; Baudelaire had rebelled and sought solace and inspiration in hashish and a Black Venus.

Laforgue represents the *fin de siècle* spirit. Although he understood and admired his predecessors, he was also aware of how puerile certain aspects of these revolts were and to what extent they were a pose. The *fin de siècle* attitude was therefore less spectacular yet no less profound. It did not have recourse to violent accusations against society nor did it, when most maturely expressed, seek originality at any price. Turning inward, it produced works of gently agitated melancholy mingled with urbane irony (often self-irony, the antidote for self-pity) and wit. This is why Laforgue felt greater kinship with Heinrich Heine than with Baudelaire. "To understand him [Baudelaire] better," he writes, "think for a moment of the opposite pole, of the sick and Christlike child, no Creole, who gave way to his crises without pose—Heine."

The gentle melancholy is that of Verlaine's "Il pleure dans mon coeur," which Laforgue expresses in "Autre Complainte de l'orgue de Barbarie:"

> —*Voyons, qu'est-ce que je veux?*
> *Rien. Je suis-t-il malhûreux!*

The young idealists possess "une belle âme / Comme on n'en fait plus aujourd'hui," and they find life so "quotidienne." But they are too civilized to rebel. They find consolation in their works, which mirror as much of their inner state as their inbred *pudeur* will permit them to display. Their language is thus less incisive than that of their predecessors, but its very oscillation between lyrical impulse and self-ironic restraint permits the reader to prolong in his mind the echo of its sound.

The Moral of the *Moralités*

William Jay Smith

"Jules Laforgue—quelle joie!" said Huysmans, and nowhere in all his work does one feel the aptness of this
remark more than in the *Moralités légendaires*. Here,
as in his final poems, Laforgue is at the height of his
inventive powers. What delight there is in these exqui-
sitely wrought tales; what flash and sparkle of youthful
genius. There is surely no prose of the late nineteenth
century that is so ornate without being heavy: it is
light to the occasional point of frivolity but somehow
always firm; it is delicate but rarely weak. Here Laforgue works within the fulness of his orbit, and only
on the sure base of sensibility could rise such intaglio
of intellect. "From the sublime to the arabesque,"
James Gibbons Huneker said of Laforgue, "is but a
semitone in his antic mood." And so in these tales he
moves, giving dimension with a quick brush-stroke to
everyday events and objects, making what is ordinary
and everyday seem fantastical and strange, and what is
strange and fantastical ordinary and everyday. While
Perseus rides off through the air to return to the "pays
élégants et faciles," Andromeda remains with the
Dragon on the "pauvre île quotidienne." And the
reader knows that she is right to remain: the Monster,
after all, is a good friend, gentleman, poet, and
scholar, who will spend hours polishing pebbles for
her in much the way that Spinoza polished his lenses.

That he becomes transformed immediately into a prince is but the final triumph of her accommodation to her routine day-to-day existence with him.

At first glance, Laforgue's purpose in the *Moralités légendaires* appears to be a stylistic one: he wishes to dispense with bombast and grandiloquence, to restore to art a sense of proportion and common sense, to wring the neck of rhetoric in his own way. But as in all his work, this stylistic purpose reflects a deeper psychological one. He began to write these tales in the fall of 1883, the first one being "Le Miracle des roses." The stories are, in a sense, a parallel development to the *Complaintes*. In the poems he attempted to cast traditional poetic and philosophical themes in common everyday popular songs; in the stories, he brings myth and lofty legend down to earth, he cuts his heroes down to size. Of course, the simplest and most direct, if not always the most effective, means of accomplishing this is through parody; indeed, the *Moralités* have been called nothing but "parodies artificielles." It is true that, at their worst, they do degenerate into a kind of schoolboy burlesque, as in "Salomé." The wit disintegrates in places, and we have a sense of the smart aleck, something gets between the author and his material, and the result is a series of monkeyshines. Even at his worst, however, Laforgue is never gross nor uncouth; the comedy almost always remains that of the drawing room rather than of the smoking car. But parody is not Laforgue's real purpose. The *Moralités* seem to point up no moral. In the brief epilogue to "Persée et Andromède," the princess who has listened to the tale exclaims to the raconteur: "Mais il n'y a jamais moyen de discuter et de s'instruire avec vous. Allons, rentrons prendre le thé. Ah! à propos, et la moralité? J'oublie toujours la moralité. . . ." Laforgue would have us forget the point, for the point is always made by indirection. The moral is as much in how the thing is said as it is in what is said. And what he says in the entire book is that all the past—history, myth, and legend—exists everywhere and for all of us: we are in it, and it is in us.

The past is a living thing, and our heroes are where we find them. Perseus, alighting from his hippogriff, might have just arrived by taxi for the *bal des quat'z-arts*:

> Persée est coiffé du casque de Pluton qui rend invisible, il a les ailes et les talonnières de Mercure et le divin bouclier de Minerve, à sa ceinture ballotte la tête de la Gorgone Méduse dont la seule vue changea en montagne le géant Atlas, comme on sait, et son hippogriffe est le Pégase que montait Bellérophon quand il tua la Chimère. Ce jeune héros a l'air fameusement sûr de son affaire.

We know exactly what to expect of him. Lohengrin appears on his taciturn, heraldic swan, "glissant, grandissant, magique, gardant sa pose, sûr de tout!" He is the essence of refinement and polish, this "jeune homme de Diane," but he is also most ineffectual; and we are not astonished when in the Nuptial Villa his pillow is transformed into a swan and he is carried back to his heavenly home. Hamlet is presented as a little creature so unimposing physically that he is scarcely even recognized at Elsinore as a royal personage.

"Poor humanity has not produced a *pure hero*," Laforgue wrote, "and all those that are cited to us in antiquity are creatures like ourselves who have been crystallized in legend—neither Buddha, Socrates, nor Marcus Aurelius—I'd like to know their daily lives."

Laforgue always had his personal and private reasons for depicting his heroes as he did: indeed, he put a great deal that is recognizably himself into his "Hamlet"; and though his heroes are at times rather hopelessly immature, they are, for all their posturing, ordinary people. In the destruction of the hero there is still something heroic that survives. With this treatment of myth, Laforgue, poetically and intuitively, hit upon a wholly modern approach; the heroes of the past must be recreated by each human consciousness in its own way; they are perpetually waiting to be reborn. It is this perception, which psychologically and artistically places Laforgue far in advance of his time, that interested James Joyce. (And we know from Padraic Colum that Joyce admired the tales early in his career.) Without the *Moralités légendaires, Ulysses* would not have been possible.

So completely did Laforgue live through his eyes that one can almost say that he saw these tales as tone poems and assigned to each of them a certain color: black to "Hamlet," red to "Le Miracle des roses," white to "Lohengrin," yellow to "Salomé," green and gold to "Pan et la syrinx," gray to "Persée et Andromède," and violet to "Les deux Pigeons," which Laforgue decided to eliminate from the book. Each story is bathed in its own color; and the reader has the sense as he proceeds of experiencing an entire scale of color values. The "Lohengrin" of Laforgue with its ice-cold lunar landscape bears many resemblances to "The Eve of St. Agnes" of Keats, and like Keats, Laforgue is aware of the emotional overtones which color can provide. The descriptive passages in the *Moralités légendaires* do not exist apart from the story; the detail, exquisite in itself, serves to move the plot forward. The landscape, in some remarkable way, actually helps to define the characters; as in a finely wrought tapestry, all is interwoven with extreme care. Salomé, in her spidery yellow muslin with its black polka dots, has a real affinity with the heavens; she is actually a manifestation of the Moon Goddess, an earthly projection of the Milky Way.

Two themes are paramount in all the tales: one is the proximity of death ("Adieu paniers, vendanges sont faites!"), the other, the permanence of art ("Vous voyez bien, vous-même; il n'y a que l'art; l'art c'est le désir perpétué"). Perhaps it is Laforgue's youth and his awareness of an early death, as well as of his own genius, that gives the tales, like the best of his poems, their special poignancy. The turning point of Lohengrin comes when the Knight-Errant turns to Elsa and says, as he caresses her in a curious, abstracted way: "Cette Villa-Nuptiale sent la fosse commune," and Elsa replies, "Nous sommes tous mortels." The grave gapes wherever Laforgue looks, and it is always attended by the beautiful goddess, Our Lady the Moon, the Moon Goddess, Death-in-Life, *la belle dame sans merci*. Ruth, the consumptive heroine of "Le Miracle des roses," wears on her breast a strange enamel medallion around which the story revolves; this medallion represents the spot of a peacock's tail resting under a human eyelid. It is thus a symbolical presentation of the Evil Eye which is inevitably linked with death: in its core of purple, it signifies here the dark of the moon. The story may be said to relate, therefore, a lunar eclipse: the Holy Sacrament representing the male symbol, the Sun, passes before the female, the Moon; and a miracle is accomplished in the brief meeting of life and death. The continued spilling of blood throughout the story has furthermore quite clear sexual connotations; in the blood of the female there is life and death. Laforgue says elsewhere

> *La Femme?*
> *—J'en sors,*
> *La mort*
> *Dans l'âme . . .*

But also attendant at the grave throughout is the artist. Hamlet is above all else an artist, a poet who seems more interested in the success of his play than in justice or revenge, and as an artist he dies: "Qualis . . . artifex . . . pereo." In "Pan et la syrinx," one of the most beautiful of the tales, the nymph is "perpetuated" on the reed flute of Pan: art is triumphant. "Pan et la syrinx" and "Persée et Andromède" appear to have been written in 1886 and 1887 after Laforgue's courtship and marriage; and both stories are more luminous, more affirmative than any Laforgue had written previously. Laforgue, the writer, like Laforgue, the artist, was more and more attached to life the nearer he came to death. The Medusa's deadly eyes close when confronted with the Dragon in "Persée et Andromède": the Medusa cannot harm an old friend. Laforgue wanted to believe that the goddess could be kind, but even in the few glorious golden days he experienced before his death—that period of elation and heightened vision so familiar to the consumptive —he was not wholly convinced: he knew that she was more often cruel. And indeed she was. But the goddess who demanded his life was also his muse, and no matter how exacting her demands, in the end he had served her well.

"A little more piety!" Laforgue exclaimed at one point. "Art is not just a schoolboy's exercise, *it is all of life.*" Art *was* life to Laforgue, and he left no better testimonial to the fact than his moral tales. Art for art's sake, yes, which meant art for life's sake as well. And how paradoxical it is that there can be so much life in a book so concerned with death, and so much freshness of spirit in a work so artificial in nature. In the notebook Laforgue kept in Berlin in 1884–85, he remarks that formerly he had seen only things themselves, but that now he had begun to see the shadows of things. The shadows are present here in the *Moralités,* and they would surely have lengthened with time.

Laforgue and Mallarmé
Robert Greer Cohn

It would be fun to sketch out a modern poet's equivalent of Shakespeare's seven ages of man, starting with
the Rimbaldian babe in the woods, awakening amid
the trembling light and shade or, a bit later, advancing
fearfully and curiously like a hop-o'-my-thumb along a
mysterious path. Then the schoolboy, and here we
might evoke Proust's little Marcel falling curls over
heels into puppy love with the Impressionist appari-
tion of Gilberte. For the lover, sighing like furnace, we
would substitute a newer kind of adolescent, prome-
nading his bitterness through the twilit suburban
springtime Sunday to the plaintive accompaniment of
pianos played by forever inaccessible *jeunes filles*. And
here, of course, we are thinking of Jules Laforgue.

In a more sober, scholarly mood, if we think of
Laforgue we are apt to think of Mallarmé, partly
because both are labelled in the manuals as Symbolists: Mallarmé is said to be the master of the so-called
school, Laforgue a tangential, fugitive, ironic, and
plainer-speaking junior member, with affinities to Corbière and, lord help us, the "Decadents." Today we
are inclined to be as impatient with such tags as the
poets, when asked, usually declare themselves to be.
But—as long as we are doing that sort of thing, and we
are sometimes forced to—if we make the term Symbolist big enough to stand for the prodigious wave of

expression—late Romantic in emotional power and classic in precision of aesthetic form—arising in the latter nineteenth and early twentieth centuries and best represented by Baudelaire, Mallarmé, Rimbaud, Valéry, Proust, Joyce, Eliot, Rilke, and a few others, then Laforgue can be said to belong in this perspective with minimal damage to his individuality.

Mallarmé was the only one of these figures Laforgue encountered personally, and he was much attracted by the older poet (eighteen years his senior) as we know from the numerous admiring references in his letters to Kahn. For example, Laforgue speaks of "those absences of syntax—the Mallarmé principle which I adore"; or he calls him "an exquisite man and a very liberal artist" and adds "what would I not give for Mallarmé to collect his poems in verse and prose in a graspable volume." Or again, "After having favored eloquent developments . . . I am becoming . . . Mallarméan." In some posthumously published critical fragments he identifies Mallarmé with his favorite philosophic principles, the "Unconscious" and the self-denying "Buddhist sage." We must allow that this was only a tentative affinity because on the one hand Laforgue was young and excessively busy, and on the other hand Mallarmé was not yet his complete self, far from it, when Laforgue read him, in the early 1880's. But starting from this promising base, it is possible and even likely that Laforgue, had he survived, would have developed the affinity further: precisely because he was a very great artist, he could not have helped responding in some important ways to the challenge that Mallarmé represented to almost every leading man of letters of the twentieth century.

This approach to the evolution of literature in the modern period is not apt to win friends these days and is usually dubbed old hat. How often have we been told that Symbolism, in any sense, is dead and that the ironic-conversational poetry and prose of Laforgue helped to kill it! The characteristic procedure in this respect is to set up a straw man of Symbolism by playing on the ambiguity of the word, referring to the school of 1885, the narrower line of epigones or minor poets, "little Symbolists" like Régnier, Vielé-Griffin, Merrill, and Kahn or else pale *fin de siècle* aesthetes such as Samain or Rodenbach. Once these easy targets are demolished, we are ready for all that came after: futurism, unanimism, dada, surrealism, imagism, neo-humanism, existentialism, or what have you. Of course, there are bright literary values in most of this, and such cultural revolts are healthy and necessary: some dead branches of Symbolism were happily blown away by the merciless fresh wind of the New Spirit. But we are aware that revolt is not sufficient, that the long-range gains come only when the rare spiritually hardy figures acknowledge the power of, and responsibly measure themselves against, the Fathers. In other words, the durable writers end by growing up, in a special—artistic—sense. Yeats is more than the slim young poet of the Celtic twilight, Proust abandons his commitment to a petty neoclassical *Putsch* in favor of something Tolstoyan, Joyce went on from the adolescent Nietzschean poses of Stephan Hero to tame them and put them in their place within a major novel. All three have acknowledged their Symbolist ancestry. Or let us take the familiar case of Eliot. If he is an important poet, and he is, it is not only or primarily because of the tones he borrowed from Laforgue. Something was needed beyond the return to popular-speech rhythms preached by Pound, or the "small dry things" by Hulme, useful as they were to a renewal and a progress. The fuller Eliot, like the fuller Mallarmé, or the fuller Laforgue that was beginning to be when he died, is the one who fuses youthful sensibility with something we must clumsily refer to as "vision"—to produce ambitious later works like the *Quartets*, the *Coup de Dés*, and the book Laforgue dreamed of in his notes. Hence it is, I suspect, that although the early Laforgue was an acknowledged presence in "Prufrock" and in "Conversation galante," or the inadequate "Figlia che Piange," it is the old *Maître*, Mallarmé, who, along with Dante and some others, haunts the aging Eliot in the shape of that "familiar compound ghost" of "Little Gidding."

Brief as it was, Laforgue's development paralleled Mallarmé's in a way that is suggestive of what might have come in that ungranted future. First, there is a distinct kinship in their primary lyric sensibilities, which is partly a matter of literary *Zeitgeist* but really goes deeper than that. The autumnal and sooty crepuscular moods which color Laforgue's most characteristic pieces, he had openly admired in some prose poems from Mallarmé's first manner: "Plainte d'automne" and "Frisson d'hiver." He was enthusiastic about the latter, particularly the lines "There are no more fields and the streets are empty, I will talk to you about our furniture." He wrote to Kahn, "I have not succeeded in making felt the melancholy of autumn afternoons. I remember a certain prose poem by Mallarmé, on autumn, *voilà*," which we might try to translate as "that's the way!" Later he qualifies this praise, not liking the ending of the prose poem. But the imagery clearly impressed him: the dying season with the overtones of universal decay and, especially, the *Orgue de Barbarie* or street organ which Mallarmé described as follows: "Yes, truly the instrument of the sad: the piano scintillates, the violin brings light to torn fibres, but the street organ, in the twilight of memory, made me desperately dream." Laforgue's "Dimanches" is a good example of this mood. Here are lines in a rough transcription:

> O, young girl at the piano!
> Fatal bouquets of memory,
> Mad and decadent legends,
> Enough! I know your tricks,
> And my soul will soon be off.
> True, a Sunday under a grey sky
> And I'm good for nothing more
> The least sound of a street organ
> (Poor beggar!) twists my entrails.

Beyond sensibility, the other main link between the two writers is that both of them early conceived of an ambitious book to embody a metaphysical or cosmic vision. This sort of experience of a plunging insight into the texture of reality seems to be the climax of the prolonged crisis of adolescence characteristic of genius, which Mallarmé referred to as the moment when the disappearing child casts forth a dazzlement and constitutes itself as the adult of either sex. With Descartes it was the illumination in the German stove-room which gave us that new syntax, analytic geometry. With Mallarmé himself, it was the Avignon crisis which produced (as we see in the fragments of "Igitur" and other notes or letters from that period) the basic structure for his Grand' Œuvre. Valéry alludes to a similar experience in his "Introduction to Descartes." Now, in the posthumous fragments of Laforgue we find the following: "And then my great book of prophecy, the new Bible, which will cause the cities to be deserted. The vanity of all, the rending apart of Illusion, the Anguish of the times, the renunciation, the uselessness of the Universe, the misery and ordure of the earth lost in vertigoes of eternal apotheoses of suns." And this: "Let us resign ourselves to knowing nothing, to being able to do nothing to the universal essence, to necessity . . . let consciousness renounce the emphemeral vanity of our planet and let it contemplate the solemn, universal and eternal and heartless swirling of the torrents of stars." We may easily think of Mallarmé's early project entitled "the Glorious Lie" and, though immeasurably more complex, the poetic constellations of *Un Coup de Dés*. All this has a familiar nineteenth-century ring: from Poe's "Eureka" through the vain procession of appearances in the poetry of Matthew Arnold with his "sad lucidity of soul"; Balzac's *Louis Lambert*, Flaubert's *Saint Antoine, Bouvard et Pécuchet*, and the unwritten work to be called *La Spirale*; Hugo's *Légende des Siècles*, Villiers, Carlyle, Ghil, the philosophers of pessimism and the unconscious, and others, *ad infinitum* and to some—those who speak of "le stupide 19e siècle"—*ad nauseam*. Laforgue does owe a great deal to these writers and thinkers, a surprising number of whom he had read; and he spontaneously shares even more with them, including the liberal amount of "bad form" or pomposity which often goes with magnanimity as distinguished from the consistently cautious formalism of smaller-mindedness. What brings him especially close to Mallarmé, however, is that he was not only a gifted thinker but, beyond any of the others mentioned, an exquisite poet. This rare combination of faculties in itself makes him a spiritual, if not brother then at least first cousin, of Mallarmé. Laforgue is certainly closer to the major Symbolists in this respect than he is to the Lautréamont-Corbière-Jarry tradition or even to poets who are said to have learned from him, like Pound, Cummings, or Williams.

It is a pertinent commentary on this kind of hesitant intransigent personality that Mallarmé, no more than Laforgue, did *not*, on the spot, publish a discursive account of his universal scheme as a lesser figure would have done. He sensed that it would take a lifetime of patience—this, incidentally, is the central message of "Prose pour des Esseintes"—to develop the formal means which, fused with the vision, would result in a full-bodied masterpiece. So Mallarmé's career is littered with the scraps of paper on which he worked out areas of that vast web of reality, clusters or constellations of interacting words, the most cooperative he could find through years of combing over the French language, always keeping in mind the total crystalline structure. From time to time, when he became too unhappy in his isolation, he would coyly detach a fragment of the web, and, rounding it off with a sonnet-form hem, release it to the few who cared. Whence certain of the denser sonnets such as "Ses purs ongles," "Une dentelle s'abolit," "A la nue accablante tu," "Au seul souci de voyager," "Quand l'ombre menaça." In a comparable—though on the whole less puristic—spirit, Laforgue produced his better poems and the finer passages of the *Moralités légendaires*, which are of enduring value because they are as original as a morning emerging from the chaos of night, freshly vibrant with the whole scheme of things he held in his Hamletic head. Mallarmé offered the *Moralités* high praise, calling them the "contes de Voltaire du Symbolisme" and obviously was sympathetic toward the poetry in verse according to a lost letter Laforgue mentions to Kahn, as well as a pretty compliment in "Crise de Vers." This lyrico-philosophic kinship of the two poets helps explain why the beginning of Laforgue's "Hamlet," despite the irony to which he clings like ivy to the battlements of Elsinore, evokes the setting of the "Ouverture ancienne" of Mallarmé's "Hérodiade": every element of this moody tableau—the solitary figure at the tower-window overlooking autumnal palace grounds, complete with swans—is found in both. Laforgue, to be sure, has strewn *his* scene with garbage; yet, *mirabile dictu,* when the Perelmanesque laughter has subsided, the beauty of the scene remains. A like similitude is found in the seascape of "Persée et Andromède," where there is the same air of comic indifference as we find on the second-to-last page of *Un Coup de Dés*, and in both texts the key words "indifféremment" and "quelconque" are used to express the listless waves, heedless of man's Icarus flight and fall.

With "Pan et la Syrinx," Laforgue turns to drowsy pastoral summer tones: as the god pursues the nymph through the sensual woods, wondering whether he had dreamed—his erotic aim frustrated and "perpetuated" in art—we are *very* close in feeling, and often in words, to Mallarmé's "L'Après-midi d'un faune," which Laforgue had read (though, as he said, hurriedly). In "Salomé" Laforgue comes equally near to a Mallarméan motif, one which was woven into the culminating work but also received unusually full treatment in separate long poems: the mysterious confrontation of Hérodiade—or Salomé—and Saint John the Baptist. In both poets' versions of the legend, the chief interest lies in a mysterious erotic relationship between the girl and the saint. And in both, the severed head on the salver surrounded by its halo (as in Gustave Moreau's painting) is seen as a new star. Irony and humor are present as ever in Laforgue, but the pain and seriousness are there too: Salomé recites a long piece containing some of Laforgue's favorite ideas on the nature of things, including this: "Man is only an insect under the skies; but let him respect himself and he is indeed God. A spasm of the creature is worth all of nature." Though we are not really interested in influences, we may be conscious that Mallarmé had read this when he wrote his sonnet "Quand l'ombre menaça" which tells us that the luxurious garlands of stars in the ebony vault of night are "only a pride denied by the darkness in the eyes of the solitary man dazzled by his faith." In the same meditation, Laforgue remarks that "the drama of the sun and death is aesthetic par excellence"; Mallarmé certainly agreed: the "double solar evolution," the "tragedy of nature," to which he alluded in a minor work of 1880, became the core of the *Coup de Dés*.

Altogether, we may say, then, that Laforgue and Mallarmé can, without more than the usual critical violence, be put in a fellowship, both in terms of lyric sensibility and the poetic "vision" which, when dialectically interfused with the verse brings about advanced lyricism, the "high symphony" Mallarmé aimed at in the *Coup de Dés* (by which metaphor he meant no hybrid creation à la Wagner, whose aesthetic he explicitly rejected, but rather ambitious poetry as poetry). Or we may think of the equivalent musical allusion and comparably ripe achievement in Eliot's *Quartets*. Laforgue, of course, did not live to attain this level of realization, but his later works point in this direction. The term Warren Ramsey borrowed from F. O. Matthiessen, the "music of ideas," indicates very appropriately the newly ambitious scope and tone of the last poems, the *Derniers Vers*. "L'Hiver qui vient," which is probably his masterpiece in verse, has a sustained seriousness which in no wise vitiates the individual Laforguian voice, on the contrary. The dry irony is there but less automatically and compulsively: it is farther than ever from the nervous rhythms of Corbière. The autumnal tone, which Laforgue had intimately exploited for its every resonance, still prevails: but now the single season, without betrayal of its intimacy, manages to stretch toward the seasonal round and the flight of years in a broader space and time; the early vision is now raised to poetic power as it was not in the abortive efforts of his first collection (*Le Sanglot de la Terre*), and Laforgue here approaches the late manner of the leading moderns. I will cite only two short excerpts which illustrate the shifting perspective; first the dying season:

> *This evening a finished sun lies at the top of the hill*
> *Lies on its side, in the broom, on its coat*
> *A white sun like spit on the floor of an estaminet*
> *On a sick-litter of yellow broom*
> *Of yellow autumn broom-bushes*
> *And the horns sound to it!*
> *He should come back*
> *He should come back to life*
> *Tally-ho tally-ho and view the death*

Lastly, the modulation into a reach of years:

> *No, No! It is the season and the foolish planet*
> *May the south wind, the south wind*
> *Ravel the boots that Time knits for itself*
> *It is the season, oh tearings, it is the season*
> *All the years through all the years*
> *I'll try in harmony to sound the tone.*

Laforgue and the Theatre

Haskell M. Block

Jules Laforgue can hardly be considered among the important French playwrights of the later nineteenth century, yet had he lived longer, he might have distinguished himself in the theatre. Laforgue was a passionate lover of the stage and had genuine aspirations as a dramatic author; but his theatrical projects largely went the way of his other ambitions in expansive and complex literary forms: the novel, epic poetry, history, philosophy, and literary criticism. In his brief but intense span of creative activity, Laforgue completed only two short dramatic compositions. These could hardly be described as representative modern plays; nevertheless, they are of high interest, both intrinsically and as part of Laforgue's poetic testament, and they have scarcely received more than passing attention, even from the poet's admirers.

Laforgue seems to have had an inherent love of spectacle and performance. Gustave Kahn relates that in 1880, when he made the acquaintance of the shy youth from Tarbes "Il m'apprit qu'il se voulait consacrer à l'histoire d'art et il méditait aussi un drame sur Savonarole." [1] Neither Kahn nor Laforgue make any further mention of this play, lost, no doubt, among the poet's "bousculante multiplicité de tentatives." [2] Still, it may have been written or, at any rate, sketched out. Referring to his early years in Paris, Laforgue remarked in 1886 in a letter to his brother,

Emile: "Je me souviens du temps où je portais à Bour- get des pièces de théâtre. . . ." [3] Most of Laforgue's early works as well as many of his later writings have disappeared, perhaps for good,[4] and we may never know what his first theatrical attempts were like. In any event, there can be no doubt of the young poet's keen and continuing interest in the drama.

It is reasonable to suppose from allusions in his writings that Laforgue knew the literary theatre of his day rather well. Shakespeare and Goethe, Musset and Banville, Wagner and Villiers de l'Isle-Adam, and perhaps many others, all helped to enlarge and enrich his experience of dramatic art. Far more important, however, for Laforgue's development than any of these literary antecedents was the theatre of the caba- ret and the music hall. Gustave Kahn has testified to his friend's ardent enjoyment of the performances of the café *fumistes* who met at the meetings of "les Hydropathes" at a cabaret on the rue de Jussieu.[5] Here poetic recitation and acrobatic clowning went hand in hand with lively topical satire, ribald improvisation, song, and dance. Established in the fall of 1878, "les Hydropathes" may well have constituted "le premier cabaret de poètes récitants." [6] Gustave Kahn has al- luded to Alphonse Allais, Maurice Rollinat, Emile Goudeau, and other performers whose *Ballades* and *Complaintes* delighted the young Laforgue.[7] The tender melancholy, playful irony, and conversational badinage of Laforgue's poetry clearly owe a great deal to these cabaret artists.[8] The image of the clown, "vêtu / D'ironie et de grâce," recurs in the mono- logues of Emile Goudeau, whose whimsical poems are marked by an air of sophistication and sentimentality: "Clown élégant qui veut qu'au public on sourie." [9] Similarly, a love of fantasy, incongruity, and the grotesque is heralded in the spirited lines of Rol- linat: [10]

Pour moi la Norme est abolie
Et j'applique en toute saison
Sur la face de la Raison
Le domino de la Folie . . .

The caprice and verve of the cabaret poets, along with
their oral style with its easy refrains, lively repetitions,
and colloquial and slang diction, must have made a
profound impression on the young Laforgue. Cabaret
performance is clearly at the root of both his lyric and
dramatic art. Later, in Berlin and London, as well as
in other foreign cultural centers, Laforgue pursued his
love of clowns, acrobats, dancers, mimes, and min-
strels.[11] His Berlin chronicles reveal a keen familiarity
with all forms of spectacle: the circus, music hall,
ballet, and café-concert, as well as the opera and the
fashionable theatre.[12] He must have seen a good many
plays in Berlin between 1881 and 1886; an entry in his
agenda for 1883 states: "le soir théâtre troupe
Meiningen," [13] and his comments on the Berlin performance of Henry Irving in *Hamlet* point unmistakably to his own playful interpretation of the role: "J'ai
trouvé cet Irving trop dramatiquement concentré
dans son masque, se prenant trop au sérieux." [14] Despite his interest in high tragedy, his preference was
plainly for popular dramatic forms, such as "le théâtre
puppazzi américain," [15] or the British music hall. An
entry in his notebooks gives further proof of the poet's
sheer delight in performance: "—Victoria theater 300
femmes sur la scène—de 6 à 40 ans.—De la chair à
ballets. Les militaires dans la salle (fête) chairs à
canon." [16] In Paris during the last months of his life,
Laforgue's theatre consisted mainly of the Opéra-Co-
mique, cabaret, mime, vaudeville, and other modes of
popular entertainment. The whimsicality and playful
irony of Pierrot, dominating Laforgue's poetry, is at
the same time a reflection of the theatre at the Gaîté

or the Bouffes-Parisiens which Laforgue knew and enjoyed.

Appropriately, the image of the clown is at the center of the first of Laforgue's plays that has been preserved, *Pierrot fumiste*, composed during the productive summer of 1882.[17] Its composition did not come easily. In a letter of August 20 the poet alluded to "une grande pièce: *Pierrot fumiste* qui me donne des convulsions." [18] It seems to have been composed —or at any rate, finished off, hastily. Squarely in the tradition of *commedia dell' arte*, the playlet probably has its immediate origins in the irreverent and farcical *saynette* of Huysmans and Hennique, *Pierrot sceptique*, published in 1881.[19] In a letter of December of that year, Laforgue asked Charles Henry: "Avez-vous lu . . . *Pierrot sceptique* de Huysmans et Hennique?" [20] Laforgue must have read it on publication, and with keen delight. *Pierrot sceptique* consists of sheer buffoonery, the ribald antics of a clown during the funeral preparations for his dead wife. He locks his tailor in a closet as an example of how to treat creditors, and the poor wretch bangs on the door all during an abortive seduction attempt in the apartment. Pierrot is nonplussed at his failure when, at the end of the scene, the tailor's skeleton flies out of the closet. The farcical pantomime is a comic spoof of bereavement that goes absolutely nowhere, but Laforgue must have enjoyed the lively earthiness of Pierrot and his affront to middle-class morality.

The same flippant and light-hearted satire characterizes *Pierrot fumiste*. The opening scene portrays the wedding procession of Pierrot and Colombinette on the steps of the Madeleine. Carefree and frivolous, Pierrot refuses to take his marriage seriously. On the wedding night he denies the full rights of marriage to his passionate but innocent wife, and persists in his refusal despite the intervention of a doctor and the mother-in-law. A suit for separation is filed and Pierrot loses, but on his last night with Colombinette he takes full advantage of his rights as a husband. As his furious love dissolves in tears, he declares:

> Je t'aimais bien; tu aurais été la plus heureuse des femmes, mais on ne m'a pas compris. Te voilà veuve irremariable. Et il partit léger et ricanant, dansant dans son compartiment à chaque station.

The long plot summary that closes the final scene suggests an ampler conception of the action, but also an impatience on the part of the author with its completion. *Pierrot fumiste* begins with mock-serious badinage and ends with a scenario. The transition from dialogue to mime is altogether in keeping with the farcical tone of the piece, but the mixture of bawdy and sentimental dialogue is so spirited and comical that one cannot help wishing the poet had not abandoned it so lightly.

Pierrot fumiste has not been taken seriously by many of Laforgue's admirers. Pierre Reboul is virtually alone in according Laforgue's "farce énorme et triste" any extended consideration,[21] but his view of the play as an expression of the poet's supposedly weak sexuality is questionable,[22] and may be flatly contradicted by the final scene. It may be that the work rose out of an abortive love affair during the early days of Laforgue's stay in Germany, but this is conjectural and immaterial. More important, we may find the same ironic and poignant comic mask in the hero of *Pierrot fumiste* as in the *Complaintes* of Lord Pierrot that constitute some of Laforgue's best poetry. Although the play is clearly unfinished, viewed within the tradition of vaudeville and cabaret performance, it cannot fairly be described as "peu dramatique."[23]

Pierrot fumiste is a striking expression of Laforgue's originality and his love of mask, mime, and farcical extravaganza, remote from any overt or tendentious preoccupation.[24] His hero points not only to *Les Complaintes*, but to the spirited and meditative clowns of Musset, Banville, Paul Margueritte, or Apollinaire. *Pierrot fumiste* is an early attempt at theatrical exploitation of the poet's characteristic gestures and devices. A slight play but one by no means mediocre for a beginner, it reveals a talent for spectacle and farce that might have led to a significant achievement in the theatre had time sufficed.

The years 1882–83 may well have been a period of intense dramatic activity for the young French poet in Berlin. Texts are lacking but from Laforgue's correspondence we know that he planned several plays during this time and worked on at least some of them. Painfully aware of the low estate of the French theatre in the early 1880's and emboldened by the composition of *Pierrot fumiste*, Laforgue envisioned a new mode of theatre, poetic and intimate, strikingly akin to Mallarmé's "obsession d'un théâtre encore réduit et miniscule ou lointain, . . . intime gala pour soi." [25] In a letter of November 18, 1882, alluding to his theatrical projects, the aspiring young playwright declared: "Et le théâtre injouable ou à jouer entre amis." [26] The conception of an unactable and intimate theatre suggests an enterprise similar to Musset's *Un Spectacle dans un fauteuil* in its playful love of fantasy and caprice, but it also points ahead to the symbolist ideal of coterie theatre that was to find fuller expression in the 1890's. In a letter of December, 1882, Laforgue mentioned the composition of a one act play "plus noire que *les Corbeaux*," [27] but nothing more is known of it, and the poet probably destroyed it. The following March he alluded to a plan for a one-act *Faust*,[28] but the work may never have proceeded beyond the first stages. It is clear, however, that Laforgue continued with his dramatic efforts, for in a letter to Charles Henry in August, 1883, he declared:

> Quant à ma pièce qui n'est point un drame ni une comédie, mais une pièce, un acte: franchement, elle me paraît maintenant un *exercice* dans ce genre avec une bonne volonté de faire autre chose que ce qu'on fait ordinairement, pas plus.[29]

Perhaps Laforgue's evident dissatisfaction here refers to *Pierrot fumiste*, but he may have had a more recent composition in mind. In view of Laforgue's persistent preoccupation with the drama and his eager search for new theatrical forms, it is surprising that more did not come of these efforts. In his self-deprecation, Laforgue seems to have refused to take his endeavors seriously, and beneath this refusal we may sense doubts concerning his dramatic talent. All of the compositions which Laforgue planned or wrote for the theatre in 1882–83 were in one act; like his poetry, Laforgue's art of the theatre was compressed, taut, economical, relying on subtlety and understatement rather than expansive speech or anecdotal narrative. Clearly, his theatrical attempts left a lasting mark on his poetic style. Warren Ramsey has commented on the dramatic impulse animating the structure of the *complainte*, with its reliance on dialogue and choral recitation.[30] The relative detachment of the poet from the words and gestures of his characters enabled him, in his best poems, to dramatize conflicts in character relationships. As Pierre Reboul has well said, "Le théâtre . . . lui imposait ce hiatus entre l'homme et l'oeuvre, qui fait une part de son originalité." [31]

By far the better known of Laforgue's two published plays, *Le Concile féerique* is in fact a composite work, formed by the grouping in dialogue form of five of the poems collected for *Des Fleurs de bonne volonté*, a volume prepared by the poet in 1886 for publication but soon abandoned.[32] Scarcely half a dozen lines in the play are new.[33] Evidently Laforgue "composed" his little play in answer to the importunities of Gustave Kahn who pressed him for contributions to his review, *La Vogue*. Laforgue mailed it to Kahn in June, 1886, but indicated that he did not consider it finished.[34] Nevertheless, Kahn published it soon afterwards in *La Vogue*, in the issues for July 12 and 19, 1886. The play also appeared in a small separate edition, and was then forgotten until the posthumous publication of *Les derniers vers de Jules Laforgue* in 1890. It is regrettable that the editors of this collection, Dujardin and Fénéon, had no manuscript of the play available to them; apparently irretrievably lost, it might have illuminated the processes by which Laforgue attempted to transform poetry into drama.

Le Concile féerique is far closer to dramatic poetry than to poetic drama. There is no plot and little characterization; simply the nocturnal musings of a man and a woman before and after their sensual embrace. The lovers are surrounded by a Chorus and an Echo, whose dialogue both masks and comments on the physical act of love. While the hero and heroine expose their inner emptiness and the vanity of earthly existence, the Chorus and Echo reduce the serious pretensions of the lovers to bitter farce. The lady's love of physical beauty has no more significance than her partner's hedonism, and during the passage of time from night to dawn, human love itself becomes the victim of Laforgue's travesty. In the parodies of Don Juan and Faust that follow the love embrace, neither the male's celebration of the pursuit of pleasure nor his partner's luxuriation in the mystery and power of the Eternal Feminine have any importance. The Echo's view of love as a meaningless rite is borne out by the final reduction of the human comedy to primitive animality, "nos bonheurs d'autochtones!" The cynical injunction of the Chorus which closes the play, "Consolez-vous les uns les autres," may be taken as a mocking invitation to the reader and spectator, as well as to the lovers, to accept the limits of the human condition in our fragile universe. The plight of the lovers is an analogue of common human experience.

Laforgue's verse proverb ultimately fuses all of the voices into a single attitude. All the characters share the same ironic sophistication, along with a keen awareness of the littleness and emptiness of even the most passionate of acts. How much farther their insight into human nature and destiny may go is difficult to say. Gustave Kahn sees a sane and prudent Epicureanism as the final wisdom of the play:

> les deux protagonistes reconnaissent que la Terre est bonne, en acceptant simplement les multiples conseils du Choeur et de l'Echo. Vivre en toute simplicité et ne plus trop creuser, vivre à la bonne franquette, selon l'illusion de fête générale et épanouie de la Dame, ou bien les tréteaux disparaîtraient pour ne plus laisser voir que des déserts gris.[35]

Kahn sees a final consolation that is real rather than ironic; however, this easy acceptance of human infirmity and inadequacy is somewhat more reassuring than the play itself might support. The bleak despair underlying the ironic vision in Le Concile féerique is not dispelled by the lovers' final acquiescence. The reward of accommodation is a pleasure of no importance: the masquerade is still an empty game.

Delightfully engaging in its wit and verve, Le Concile féerique is much too slight to carry any profound philosophical weight. Essentially a lyrical meditation, its lines could be reassigned without undue incongruity. The action is untheatrical and virtually static, and one may wonder if the poet envisaged the work as more than a literary exercise.[36] Unquestionably, there is a significant advance in Laforgue's transposition of isolated poems from *Des Fleurs de bonne volonté* into his playlet, but the integration is artificial. The characters are mere types, and their essential relationships are not with each other but with the cosmos. What unity the work possesses lies not in traditional dramatic elements but in a wonderful coalescence of mood and language, in which the witty and ironic commentary of the supernatural observers corresponds perfectly to the behavior of the lovers and to the lovers' insight into their own condition.

It is patently unfair to read or envision Laforgue's play from the same standpoint as a modern drama of contemporary life. The capricious make-believe, ribald farcicality, and ironic sophistication that we find permeating Laforgue's poetry and earlier play are central to his dramatic art. Despite external differences, *Le Concile féerique* is not as far removed in style and tone from *Pierrot fumiste* as one may at first glance imagine. William Jay Smith is quite right in viewing *Le Concile féerique* as akin to ballet or to cabaret entertainment: "one can well imagine a dance orchestra playing in the wings."[37] Voices take the place of gestures in a setting so bare and simple that the physical stage and its attendant properties hardly seem relevant.

Was *Le Concile féerique* actually written for the stage? The absence of almost any change in the transposition from the lyric to the dramatic mode may offer convincing proof of the intrinsically dramatic character of Laforgue's poetry with its complex interplay of several voices; but poetic drama cannot be equated with dramatic poetry. In defense of Laforgue, it should be recognized that the French theatre of the nineteenth century occasionally tolerated brief scenes or playlets in verse, either as curtain-raisers or as interludes. Camille Mauclair referred flatly to *Le Concile féerique* as "cette saynète philosophico-lyrique, injouable"; [38] but even this unsympathetic description may point to a theatrical as well as literary tradition underlying Laforgue's conception of his play.

In the middle years of the nineteenth century *Le Concile féerique* probably would have been accepted as similar in form and spirit to such compressed dramatized proverbs as Musset's *Il faut qu'une porte soit ouverte ou fermée* or the dramatic odes Banville composed for "performance" by Rachel at the Comédie Française. Banville, whose influence on Mallarmé and the symbolists was incalculable, insisted in his criticism as well as in his dramatic compositions on the need for the theatre to return to its lyrical origins: "le théâtre ne trouvera chez nous sa forme définitive que lorsque nous aurons su, comme les anciens, associer le chant et l'ode au dialogue dramatique." [39] Theatre as Banville conceives it is "la poésie dramatique mêlée de poésie lyrique, de chant." [40] It was largely in response to Banville's exhortation and example that the young Mallarmé first composed his "L'Après-midi d'un faune" in 1865 as "un intermède héroique" for performance at the Comédie Française.[41] the piece was rejected, but some years later, in seeking for ways to support himself in Paris, Mallarmé again thought of writing verse playlets for the theatre, and was bluntly informed by Catulle Mendès, "Les saynettes poétiques ne sont pas jouées." [42] All the same, it is reasonable to suppose that the verse playlet survived in the popular theatre and in the cabaret long after it had all but vanished from the more fashionable stage.

The revival of the one act play in verse was among the central preoccupations of those symbolist poets and playwrights who helped to shape the art theatre of the 1890's. The special importance of Laforgue's *Le Concile féerique* lies not only in its unique place among the poet's compositions, but in its curious history after his death, as part of the effort to create a symbolist drama. The theoretical justification for this effort was provided by the programmatic "Notes sur le théâtre" contributed by Mallarmé to the *Revue Indépendante* in 1886–87. Mallarmé viewed his essays as part of "une campagne dramatique," designed to bring the theatre into intimate accord with the principles and values of symbolist poetry.[43] "Le Théâtre," Mallarmé declared, "est d'essence supérieure"; [44] like poetry, it is the suggestion or evocation of the hidden spiritual meaning of the universe. Mallarmé's appeal for a drama of musicality and mystery was not lost on his young disciples. In an important essay of 1889, Gustave Kahn urged the implementation of a poetic conception of the theatre, expressive of "notre tissu mélodique de phrases et la position plastique de nos pensées." [45] Kahn envisioned a theatre of "milieu indéfini," marked by pantomime, ballet, "évocation de décors," and drawing upon popular as well as literary modes of theatrical expression. Kahn was one of the early *animateurs* of the symbolist drama, and in all likelihood, it was his keen and genuine appreciation of Laforgue's art that led to the performance of *Le Concile féerique.*

The Théâtre d'Art, founded by Paul Fort in 1890, constituted a deliberate effort to create a symbolist theatre.[46] Fort envisaged the new drama as essentially poetic, free from dependence on external action or spectacle: "La parole crée le décor comme le reste." [47] Frankly experimental, the Théâtre d'Art encouraged the young adherents of Mallarmé to write for the stage. In a public letter of February, 1891, Fort declared: "Le Théâtre d'Art va devenir . . . absolument symboliste." [48] Despite these high aspirations, the progress of the new theatre was slow and difficult; a repertory of symbolist drama was lacking and, like its successor, the Théâtre de l'Œuvre, the Théâtre d'Art was essentially a theatre in search of playwrights and plays appropriate to its aims. Paul Fort achieved his most significant early success with the performance of Maeterlinck's *L'Intruse* in May, 1891,[49] at a program which also included verse plays in one act by Banville, Mendès, and Verlaine. From its inception, symbolist drama was lyric drama, a brief and concentrated suggestion or evocation of ultimate spiritual mysteries.

A verse play in one act, philosophical in tone, Laforgue's *Le Concile féerique* must have seemed wholly appropriate for performance by the Théâtre d'Art. It was presented at the Théâtre Moderne on December 11, 1891, at a program consisting of five pieces, four of which were in one act. The main attraction was Maeterlinck's *Les Aveugles*; the other pieces, in addition to Laforgue's, were Remy de Gourmont's *Théodat*; *La Geste du Roy*, a series of recitations from medieval poetry; and the synaesthetic extravaganza of P.-N. Roinard, *Le Cantique des Cantiques.*[50] Laforgue's piece came fourth on a rather long program. It was directed by Adolphe Retté, who also served as prompter.[51] Retté had assisted Kahn in the editing of *La Vogue*, and shared his colleague's enthusiasm for Laforgue's work. For the occasion, Retté contributed an elaborate program note on the play, subsequently reprinted in *Le Livre d'Art*, the review and publicity organ of the Théâtre d'Art.[52] The program note is important, for it reveals that the producers of *Le Concile féerique* did not view the work as constituting " 'du théâtre' au sens que l'on donne généralement à ce mot mais bien une ode dialoguée où se retrouvent mêlés . . . ce lyrisme rêveur et cette ironie sentimentale, caractères essentiels du talent de Laforgue." Plainly, the performance was an act of tribute to the genius of the short-lived poet, hailed by Retté as "l'une des plus brillantes personnalités de l'école symboliste à son début." Recent students of Laforgue's art have qualified this judgment, emphasizing the differences in style and technique between Laforgue and the symbolists,[53] but the concreteness and objectivity of his art were perhaps less apparent in the last century than they are today. Even the most casual reading should indicate that *Le Concile féerique* is altogether different in mood and tone from *L'Intruse* or *Les Aveugles*. Seized on by the symbolists, Laforgue's play was out of place in their repertoire.

It is difficult to imagine why so urbane and amusing a piece as *Le Concile féerique* should have almost created a riot in the theatre. Retté, observing the turbulence from the prompter's box, stated that the first shouts from the spectators came from defenders of the play, aroused by neighboring mutterings of impatience, and from enemies of the hostile critic, Francisque Sarcey, who were baiting and insulting him.[54] The verbal battle did not get out of hand, and the actors were able to continue to the end; but newspaper reviewers made much of the episode. Thus an unsympathetic critic in *Le Figaro* declared:

Le public ayant paru déconcerté par des vers aux rimes bizarres et étonné par une situation incompréhensible, quelques personnes protestèrent, les imprudentes! Un coup de sifflet ayant retenti, les poètes manifestèrent. Ce fut terrible.[55]

With all due allowance for journalistic exaggeration, the restrained and seemingly innocuous playlet of Laforgue evidently did give rise to violent reactions.

Henri Fouquier reported that the defenders of the play rose en masse and threw the dissidents out of the theatre, shouting "A la porte les gens d'esprit!" [56]

Owing in part to its stormy reception, Le Concile féerique did not go unnoticed in the periodical press. No doubt, some of the reviewers overemphasized the reaction of the audience at the expense of discussion of the work itself, and more than one critic seized on the occasion to attack the very enterprise of the Théâtre d'Art. Sarcey, the acknowledged arbiter of the drama of his time, complained bitterly in his column in Le Temps of the length of the program:

> C'est un programme, cela, j'espère! Aussi la représentation n'a-t-elle été achevée qu'à une heure et demie du matin, et quelle représentation! Oh! ma tête! ma tête! [57]

Sarcey, for whom even Maeterlinck was merely "un fumiste," could make absolutely nothing out of what he called Laforgue's "tapage incessant de rimes bizarres." "Le toile tombe," he concludes in his review, "et l'on siffle." Sarcey's lack of imaginative sympathy could have been predicted, but friendlier critics, such as François de Nion of La Revue Indépendante, also felt that the program was overloaded, uneven, and dragged out, and viewed the performance of Laforgue's play as an error in judgment on the part of Paul Fort.[58] The quality of the acting, described by one critic as "bien grossière," plainly did not aid the cause of the Théâtre d'Art.[59]

Amid the considerable critical attention given to the performances of the evening, some perceptive appreciation of Le Concile féerique may be found. Julien Leclerq, writing in the Mercure de France, had high praise for Laforgue's play, finding that its simplicity and freshness contrasted markedly with the esoteric and complicated serious works on the program: "Cette fantaisie mieux qu'amusante, à qui manque l'étendue d'une oeuvre dramatique, est une page exquise d'ironique cruellement rieur dont le désir ne fut pas d'écrire pour la scène." [60] Laforgue's total indifference to stage performance may be doubted, but in any event, his aims and methods were hardly of the Théâtre d'Art. The verve and wit of Laforgue's lines must have escaped many of the spectators. As Henri Bressac declared in *L'Ermitage*, "l'art de Jules Laforgue est tellement en nuances, avec ses sursauts d'idées et d'expressions, son mélange d'ironie senti-mentale et de rêve triste, qu'il est presque impossible de le réaliser sur la scène, tant il exige d'absolues conditions de recueillement." [61] Perhaps under more suitable conditions of performance, the lyrical and meditative values of the poetry would have had a more favorable reception. For those who knew and admired Laforgue's genius, the performance of *Le Concile féerique* called renewed attention to the in-herently dramatic and theatrical character of the poet's art.

Laforgue's best known single work, *Hamlet*, reflects this intimate awareness of the theatre's ways and means. A scenario as well as a *nouvelle*, it brings together soliloquy, gesture, and dramatic dialogue in depicting the vivid interplay of the real and make-be-lieve. Hamlet is himself both actor and playwright, seeing life and art as performance and masquerade.[62] Laforgue's *Hamlet* cries out for dramatic presentation; a skillful craftsman could turn it into an effective play. Jean-Louis Barrault performed the leading role in Charles Granval's adaptation of Laforgue's work in 1939, and there have since been other adaptations and performances.[63] In structure as well as style, *Hamlet* testifies brilliantly to the steady growth of dramatic power in Laforgue's art.

It would be over-generous to consider Jules Laforgue a great playwright *manqué,* but his love and understanding of histrionic performance helped significantly to shape and direct his poetic talent. His theatrical compositions were inspired not so much by grandiose ambition as by the desire to write something striking and new. The quest for novelty and originality made Laforgue a precursor of much that is modern in twentieth century poetry. It also might have led him to imaginative and arresting discoveries in the modern drama.

The Rest is Silence: Hamlet as Decadent

Peter Brooks

Paris in the 1880's and 1890's was a city of the theatre, and its favorite play was *Hamlet*. Not only the greatest actor of the age, but also the greatest actress played the role: Mounet-Sully in 1886 and again in 1896, Sarah Bernhardt in 1899. One may assume that Sarah Bernhardt's performance *en travesti* marked the decadence of the Romantic interpretation of Hamlet—the pale, consumptive adolescent with black cloak and white plume illustrated by Delacroix. Her production excited enthusiastic controversy, and the *Revue Blanche* was able to publish a series of "Singular and Curious Opinions Concerning Lord Hamlet" by such contributors as Rachilde, Alfred Jarry, Max Nordau, J.-E. Blanche, and Beerbohm Tree.[1] But the man of this generation most haunted by Hamlet, Mallarmé, did not live to see this production, and his considerations on the Shakespearean hero date from the more Gallic versions of 1886 and 1896. Mounet-Sully played the Hamlet provided by Meurice and Claretie which, although not as faulty as the old Dumas translation—in which Hamlet lives on at the end of the play, the villains having been routed by the return of the Ghost—was considerably truncated. Its unpardonable sin—one which led Louis Ménard to brand its authors "romantico-bourgeois"[2]—was the omission of the part of Fortinbras: after the silence of the Prince, there was no peal of ordnance to signal the return of order to the body politic.

In response to an *enquête* by the *Revue Blanche,* both Lugné-Poe, of the Théâtre de l'Œuvre, and Mallarmé emphasized the dramatic necessity of Fortinbras to the play. For Mallarmé, he functions as counterpoint to the inactive dreamer: "Alors placé, certes, comme contraste à l'hésitant, Fortinbras, en tant qu'un général . . ." [Thus placed, to be sure, as contrast to the hesitating, Fortinbras, as a general . . .].[3] After the extraordinary array of unnatural deaths brought on by the Prince, Shakespeare seeks a return to normal existence in "vidant la scène avec ce moyen de destruction actif, à la portée de tous et ordinaire, parmi le tambour et les trompettes" [emptying the stage with this active means of destruction, ordinary and within everyone's reach, amidst drums and trumpets] (p. 1564). Mallarmé insists, however, that neither Fortinbras nor any of the other secondary characters should be allowed to assume a real identity, but must rather remain shadowy bit-players in the background: "Le héros—tous comparses, il se promène, pas plus, lisant au livre de lui-même, haut et vivant Signe; nie du regard les autres" [The hero—all bit players, he walks, nothing more, reading in the book of himself, high and living Sign; with his glance denies the others] (p. 1564).

Such an effacement of all secondary characters indicates to Mallarmé that Shakespeare's play points toward the theatre of the future, where action will be absorbed in monologue: "La pièce, un point culminant du théâtre, est, dans l'oeuvre de Shakespeare, transitoire entre la vieille action multiple et le Monologue ou drame avec Soi, futur" [The play, a culminating point of the theatre, is, in Shakespeare's works, transitional between the old multiple action and the

Monologue or drama with the Self of the future] (p. 1564). Such a drama demands, not characters in the ordinary sense of the term, but living symbols: "dans l'idéale peinture de la scène tout se meut *selon une réciprocité symbolique des types entre eux ou relativement à une figure seule*" [in the ideal representation of the stage, everything moves *according to a symbolic reciprocity of types among themselves or relative to one figure*].[4] *Hamlet* seems to Mallarmé a clear prefiguration of a Symbolist drama which he and some of his contemporaries hoped to perfect, if only within "the sole theatre of our mind" (p. 300). In his critical writings, the theatre, and the ballet as a super-stylized form of theatre, occupy a privileged position: "the theatre is of essence superior."[5] His "Hérodiade" was begun as a dramatic tableau, "l'Après-midi d'un faune" as a monologue to be performed by Coquelin at the Théâtre Français, "Igitur" resembles a Hamletic soliloquy and, finally, *Le Livre*, the great unrealized work, was, as far as one can tell, to have been read by an "opérateur" at a series of performances of marked dramatic solemnity.[6]

The techniques for realizing a Symbolist drama where types, symbols, affronted one another or a central personage alone characterized, were probably only discovered by W. B. Yeats. Starting from Ezra Pound's research into the Japanese Nōh theatre, he created with the masks and formalized motions of such a play as *The King of the Great Clock Tower* a dramatization of the Salomé legend which would have received Mallarmé's enthusiastic approval. The attempts of Mallarmé's own generation seem less successful: the estrangement of the Symbolists and Decadents from the actualities of the theatre was total, and Villiers de l'Isle-Adam, in his public reading of *Axël* (billed on the poster as a "new dramatic literature") declared: "It suffices to say that the drama of *Axël* is in no sense written for the stage, and that the very idea of its being produced seems to the author himself almost inadmissible." [7] It was in the logic of this theatre of the mind that it should retreat into Axël's castle. Villiers' own play, despite its many appealing qualities, often seems an abstract, undramatic rewriting of *Hamlet*, one in which the vital interplay of characters we find in Shakespeare has been frozen into the Sara-Axël-Kaspar triangle. Amidst the metaphysical and occultist claptrap, Axël at his best sounds like a *fin de siècle* Hamlet: "Contempler les ossements, c'est se regarder au miroir" [To look at bones is to stare at oneself in the mirror].[8] Villiers showed considerable insight on his relationship to Shakespeare when he announced his play was written for those who "don't consider the famous monologue of Hamlet, 'To be or not to be,' simply a *longueur*." [9]

Rather than the reaction to a precise state of affairs in Denmark, "To be or not to be" became a general debate on the relative virtues of the *ici-bas* and the *au-delà*, and the subject, as well as the monologic form of *Hamlet* was a natural theme for Symbolists and Decadents. Mallarmé captures both aspects of *Hamlet*'s appeal in an involuted phrase when he suggests that the play "semble le spectacle même pourquoi existent la rampe ainsi que l'espace doré quasi moral qu'elle défend, car il n'est point d'autre sujet, sachez bien: l'antagonisme de rêve chez l'homme avec les fatalités à son existence départies par le malheur" [seems the very spectacle for which the proscenium, and the quasi-moral gilded space which it protects, exist: for, be assured, there is no other subject: the antagonism of man's dream with the fatalities of existence allotted to him by ill fortune] (p. 300). The problem of Hamlet, to Mallarmé and his contemporaries, is that of the man who has renounced the world in a search for the ideal and the absolute, for an hermetic space, for *le rêve* in the sense of the useless yet creative and even sacred day-dreaming described in the closing sonnet of the *Poésies*, "Mes bouquins refermés sur le nom de Paphos." *Hamlet* is the exteriorization of an inner tragedy, "intimate and occult," whose hero, in his stage presence, "struggles beneath the evil of appearing" (p. 299).

In interpreting Hamlet's problem as that of "appearing," Mallarmé is shifting the locus of the Shakespearean problem: Hamlet is no longer the man who cannot decide whether or not to act, whether to obey the dictates of justice and filial piety or to renounce the struggle in death, but rather one who has opted for a life of immobile dream and now finds his vocation thwarted, his pure world violated, by the necessity to act. He is forced from the realm of pure Being into that of becoming, from necessity into contingency. Hamlet's black cloak is "the mourning he chooses to wear" (p. 299), a conscious symbol of his renunciation of existence and, despite the dénouement of the plot, his inviolability—like Axël's—is unscathed at death, "jewel intact amidst the disaster" (p. 301). As solitary protagonist in a drama become monologue, he acts with and upon shadowy objectifications of his various possible selves, and his destruction of them suggests the ferocity with which he defends his purity. Mallarmé's example is the killing of Polonius:

> Qui erre autour d'un type exceptionnel comme Hamlet, n'est que lui, Hamlet: et le fatidique prince qui périra au premier pas dans la virilité, repousse mélancoliquement, d'une pointe vaine d'épée, hors de la route interdite à sa marche, le tas de loquace vacuité gisant que plus tard il risquerait de devenir à son tour, s'il vieillissait.

[Whoever circles about an exceptional being like Hamlet is only himself, Hamlet: and the prophetic prince who will perish at his first step in manhood, with a vain sword's point melancholically pushes from the path forbidden to him, the pile of loquacious vacuity he would risk becoming himself if he grew old] (p. 301). The blow of the sword abolishes the contingencies of existence.

Mallarmé describes a version of *Hamlet* seen in his youth, billed, with an excess of French clarity, as *Hamlet, ou le Distrait*. It is from this state of distraction, of absentness, more than from madness, that Hamlet the inactive dreamer causes the death of eight people by the time the play is done: "il tue indifféremment ou, du moins, on meurt. La noire présence du douteur cause ce poison, que tous les personnages trépassent:sans même que lui prenne toujours la peine de les percer, dans la tapisserie" [he kills indifferently, or, at any rate, people die. The black presence of the doubter is cause of this poison, that all the characters die: without his always taking the trouble to run them through behind the arras] (p. 1564). For Mallarmé, the symbolism of this massacre accomplished without killing is clear: the play ends in a "somptueuse et stagnante exagération de meurtre . . . autour de Qui se fait seul" [sumptuous and stagnant exaggeration of murder . . . around Whoever makes himself alone] (p. 1564). Death—for self and for all that cross his path—is the price paid to preserve the dream: just as, in Yeats' terms, decapitation is the price paid by the poet for the perfection of his work of art. That Hamlet, facing a world of flux, impurity, corrupt mortality, should himself die is expected; but his refusal to live— in the sense of live by acting—further has the effect of piling high the corpses of others. This central irony of the role of Hamlet could not fail to appeal to Mallarmé: it transforms the impotent dreamer into a destructive ideal like Baudelaire's sacred and profane Goddess of Beauty. Villiers has his Hamlet skewer a representative figure from the outside world who has attempted to violate the cerebral virginity of the castle, and Axël makes it clear that, without lifting a finger, he can precipitate into mysterious caverns, bottomless traps, anyone attempting an attack on the bastion deep in the Schwarzwald. The thought that the exiled dreamer could abolish all the world's meddling bourgeois Poloniuses, Rosenkrantzes and Guildensterns, as well as the specifically guilty King and Queen, was exhilarating.

Stephen Dedalus—who as an artist has close affinities with the Decadents and Symbolists—returns to this aspect of *Hamlet* when discussing the play in the Dublin National Library, in the "Scylla and Charybdis" episode of *Ulysses*. A line from Mallarmé comes to him as he speaks:

> Sumptuous and stagnant exaggeration of murder.
> —A deathsman of the soul Robert Greene called him, Stephen said. Not for nothing was he a butcher's son wielding the sledded poleaxe and spitting in his palm. Nine lives are taken off for his father's one, Our Father who art in purgatory. Khaki Hamlets don't hesitate to shoot. The bloodboltered shambles in act five is a forecast of the concentration camp sung by Mr. Swinburne.[10]

Stephen, who identifies Shakespeare's point of view as that of Hamlet *père*, the ghost, sees in Hamlet the weakness of character which leads to totalitarian political murder. The massacre of Act V is not inevitable: it is the result of a son's failure to act immediately in response to a clear filial duty, of his elaborate indifference to the general death he unleashes while meditating the awful consequences to self and psyche of despatching one guilty man. Stephen's interpretation is of course dictated by his own sense of guilt for the rejection of father, and his search for a paternal replacement. It is his hatred for his father and his ambivalent feelings toward his mother which make him revert, also, to Hamlet's rantings to Ophelia: "in the economy of heaven, foretold by Hamlet, there are no more marriages, glorified man, an androgynous angel, being a wife unto himself" (p. 213). The coitus which produced them haunts both Hamlet and Stephen, the former because it was subsequently tainted by his mother's adultery, the latter because it was blind, base, unwitting; and both because their responsibilities to a father are posited on defilement of a mother. All the corruptions of the world can be traced to this original corruption in conception, and Stephen follows Hamlet's logic to the conclusion that paternity is a "legal fiction" (p. 207). The androgynous condition, which would eliminate the defilement of mother by father and the torture of filial responsibility has obvious relevance to Stephen's problems; it also exercised a wide appeal for Decadent writers: the androgynous Rachilde was a popular Parisian phenomenon, and Mallarmé's "enfant d'une nuit d'Idumée" was a poem produced by the poet's painful self-fertilization. The Decadent insistence upon purity, with its accompanying sterility, made the fecundation of self the only means of generation, and Mallarmé's theory and practice of the symbol depends upon the internal cross-fertilization of different elements of a poem, which creates, gives birth to something resembling that celebrated flower of the "Prose pour des Esseintes," an organic, self-sufficient dominant image.

Hamlet, the play and the personage, contain, if properly interpreted, so many essential Decadent themes so well dramatized that there was a natural tendency on the part of Mallarmé to think that the role and its embodiment would die with his generation: "il convenait, une fois, après l'angoissante veille romantique, de voir aboutir jusqu'à nous résumé le beau démon, au maintien demain peut-être incompris, c'est fait" [it was fitting that once, after the agonizing Romantic wake, the beautiful daemon whose attitude will perhaps not be understood tomorrow, should, in essential form, come down to us; this has been accomplished] (p. 302). Hamlet, the extra-rational dreamer in quest of an extra-temporal, imperishable world, took on, for Mallarmé and his contemporaries, all the prestige of myth: *"Le seigneur latent qui ne peut devenir,* juvénile ombre de tous, ainsi tenant du mythe" [*The latent lord who cannot become,* youthful shade of us all, thus partaking of myth] (p. 300). Like Herodias or Saint Anthony, Hamlet was a symbol of the inviolable mind of the artist, one whose long history and multiple significations authorized the elevation to the status of myth. The superiority of Hamlet to Herodias or Saint Anthony has been suggested: he is a metaphysical dreamer whose renunciation is hyperconscious; he not only rejects the world of contingency, he causes its bloody demise; haunted by the corruption of generation, he predicts a future state of androgynous creative beings; he is the exponent of pure theatre, or monologue. But, whereas Flaubert, Mallarmé, and Oscar Wilde all produced lasting versions of Herodias, and the first produced a monumental Saint Anthony, *Axël* and the fragmentary "Igitur" stand as an insufficient monument to the myth of Hamlet: their excessively metaphysical themes and language largely vitiate their value as works of art with a mythic force.

The Hamlet of Jules Laforgue—one who is aware of

his own mythic function: "Plus tard, on m'accusera d'avoir fait école" [Later they will accuse me of having started a movement] [11]—seems a more promising figure. A theme which emerges from the verbal acrobatics of all the *Moralités légendaires* is the quest for purity and eternity, variously pursued by Syrinx fleeing Pan, Salomé decapitating Iaokannan, Lohengrin escaping the seductions of Elsa on his pillow become a swan. For Laforgue's Hamlet, Ophelia's impurity is not merely the inevitable taint received from a world where whoredom is rife, but a product of her wearing of *décolleté* dresses: "Or, on le sait, la virginité des épaules, c'est tout pour moi, je ne transige jamais là-dessus" [And it is well-known that the virginity of the shoulders is everything for me; I never compromise on that] (p. 54). Ophelia is all too human: the sacrifice of the virginity of her shoulders is a prefiguration of her inevitable deflowerment by Fortinbras. She is a symbol of the corruption which has descended upon all womankind with Gertrude's fall, and this Hamlet, in imitation of Shakespeare's "Get thee to a nunnery," cries out that the "Categorical Imperative" must be replaced by the "Climacteric Imperative" (p. 24), a wish that seems to call for the androgynous state Stephen Dedalus finds predicted in Hamlet.

Laforgue's and Shakespeare's Hamlets are cursed in not having Saras with whom they can cry, "vierges encore, nous nous sommes cependant à jamais possédés" [virgins still, we have nonetheless possessed one another forever.] [12] The corruption of their women, however, is itself symbolic of the more general corruption of a rank and festering earth. Denmark is rotten, the time is out of joint, and Hamlet's refusal to set it right implicates him in the carnage. Laforgue's character does not share the indifference of Mallarmé's to the exaggeration of murder; even more than Shakespeare's Hamlet, he is haunted by blood. In a passage which surely parodies the famous hunting expedition in Flaubert's *Légende de St.-Julien l'hospitalier,* he sets out on a senseless killing of animals which tends to prove that "tout est permis—et pour cause, nom de Dieu!—contre les êtres bornés et muets" [everything is permitted—and with good reason, in the name of heaven!—against mute and narrow-minded creatures] (p. 39). His remorse for the act is quickly overcome in a consideration of the universality of blood and corruption: "Bah! ai-je été assez ridicule! Et les guerres! Et les tournées d'abattoir des siècles du monde antique, et tout! Piteux provincial! Cabotin! Pédicure!" [Bah! I am being thoroughly ridiculous! And wars! And the slaughterhouse circuits of antiquity, and all! Lamentable provincial! Clown! Chiropodist!] (p. 40). But the *hantise du sang,* the revulsion by morality and decay, remain. The theme is stated at the outset, in the description of the stagnant bay below the castle walls, and approaches the point of agony in the graveyard scene, which is as highly wrought as Shakespeare's. Yorick's skull moves Hamlet to search the world over for "the most adamantine techniques of embalming" (p. 49); he concludes that all's well that has no end at all.

There is, in Laforgue's *Moralité,* a real sense of a person unhinged by the brutality and uncleanliness of the world, and by the fact of death itself. Hamlet's incapacity to live is that of the man who has discovered the world is all either slaughterhouse or charnel house, and its pathetic expression is "Où trouver le temps pour se révolter contre tout cela?" [Where can I find the time to rebel against all that?] (p. 53). This response goes beyond the *ennui* of an Axël and rejoins Shakespearean tragedy; yet it is transmuted by the Decadent sensibility in such a line as "Stabilité! Sta-

bilité! ton nom est Femme . . . J'admets bien la vie à
la rigueur. Mais un héros!" [Stability! Stability! thy
name is Woman . . . I admit life as a last resort. But a
hero!] (p. 23). It is the stability of fragility that tor-
tures this Hamlet: the monotonous omnipresence of
corrupted and enslaved women, of corrupting and
murderous men, of ignoble ends and means and passions, finishing in the absurdity of death. Life is tenta-
tively, tenuously livable, but the idea of acting a hero's
role in such a world is absurd; merely to reflect upon
action is to go the way of madness. He has discovered
that the realm of transcendent reality in which Mallarmé's inviolable Hamlet moved is an illusion, and
his answer is to quote "Words, words, words." "Ah!
que je m'ennuie donc supérieurement!" [Ah! how su-
periorly bored I am!] (p. 50) is the cry of a self-
mocker who has come face to face with nothingness.
In his rejections, Laforgue's character resembles the
intellectual Hamlet dramatized by Valéry after the
First World War—one who sees all Europe as a vast
"terrasse d'Elsinore," an enormous graveyard where
the skulls thrown up turn out to be those of Leibniz,
Kant, Leonardo, and other major thinkers of Western
civilization.[13]

To both Laforgue and Valéry, Hamlet is a figura-
tion of the nihilistic philosopher revolted by what
man has done to his civilization. Further, to Laforgue
—as, perhaps, also to Mallarmé—Hamlet is an author,
a Decadent artist of a developed symbolizing faculty,
an unwilling man of public affairs who would prefer to
quit Elsinore for the Montagne Sainte-Geneviève
where a school of Neo-Alexandrians flourishes.
Whereas the original Hamlet inserted "some dozen or
sixteen lines" in the players' text, Laforgue's character
is author of the whole production, his "immaculate
conception" (p. 30). One of the passages he quotes

for the benefit of Kate and William expresses the essence of the problem of Hamlet the artist:

> *Un coeur rêveur par des regards*
> *Purs de tout esprit de conquête!*
> *Je suis si exténué d'art!*
> *Me répéter, quel mal de tête! . . .*
> > *O lune de miel,*
> > *Descendez du ciel!*

[A heart, dreamer by glances / Pure of any will to conquest! / I am so worn out by art! / To rehearse, what a headache! . . . / O honey moon, / Descend from heaven!] (p. 32). Being "exténué d'art," Hamlet cannot rehearse his part, cannot act, but only record. In the pleasure of writing his play, he gradually forgets the murdered father it commemorates, and the vengeance its subject matter demands. His fondness for repeating "Words, words, words" indicates both his rejection of metaphysics and his retreat into literature as an escape from the necessity to act. This has scriptural authority:

> *Why, what an ass am I! This is most brave*
> *That I, the son of a dear father murder'd,*
> *Prompted to my revenge by heaven and hell,*
> *Must, like a whore, unpack my heart with*
> > *words . . .*
> > > (Hamlet, II, ii, 547–50)

The *cabotin,* poor player as monologist, pays himself off with words; acting replaces action. Verbalization becomes his sole effort, and when the play clearly reveals the guilt of the King, Hamlet decides, "Enfin, ils sont assez punis comme ça, c'est mon avis. Moi, je file!" [In any case, they are punished enough like that in my opinion. I'm clearing out!] (p. 67). And his deathcry of "*Qualis artifex pereo!*" shows that his unrealized artistic talents are uppermost in his mind at

the last. Laforgue, like Edmund Wilson, here seems
to suggest that the art of the Decadents is a retreat
from a reality which they are psychologically incapa-
ble of confronting.

But this, as always with Laforgue, is only half the
truth; to conclude that he is invalidating the Decadent withdrawal from life would be a mistake. The
cocasserie of his hero—brother of Yorick and spiritual
cousin of Pierrot—and the irony to which he is sub-
jected, are first of all means of putting into sophisticated perspective the nonessential attributes of a Decadent ethos, so disassociating himself from the claptrap of its sensibility. Laertes—man of action and
hence villain—becomes a social worker who interests
himself in subsidized housing projects; the gravedigger
announces that the decadence of Denmark has caused
him to put all his money in Norwegian bonds, antici-
pating the arrival of Fortinbras and the barbarians; on
the next-to-last page the narrator realizes—too late!—
that Laertes, not Hamlet, should have been his hero
all along. This modernization and parody of *Hamlet*
have, further, the more important effect of bringing to
the surface—and only sometimes ridiculing—submerged suggestions Laforgue found in the Hamlet
myth. When at the outset he suggests that Hamlet's
aberrations have their origin in the discovery that
stones dropped from the castle windows into the moat
might just as well (given the reflection) be said to be
dropped into the sky, Laforgue is both mocking and
affirming the essentially metaphysical interpretation
given to Hamlet by his century. Irony, parody, and
comedy accomplish what Villiers, with his abstract
rephrasing of Hamletic problems, sought unsuccess-
fully: a remarkable lucidity, a play of light which
permits Laforgue to examine not only Hamlet himself, but the whole range of interpretation of the

myth. When Hamlet cries, "Mais ce soir il faut agir, il faut s'objectiver! En avant par-dessus les tombes, comme la Nature!" [But tonight I must act, I must objectify myself! Onward with Nature across the graves!"] (p. 36), a wide spectrum of interpretation and self-interpretation is suggested. The Hegelian language of the first sentence reminds us of the Mallarméan view of Hamlet as the "latent lord" who cannot become an objective being, while it also, in its contrast to "O from this time forth / My thoughts be bloody, or be nothing worth!," reemphasizes the pallid quality of this modern hero. The second sentence, echoing Goethe, sounds like mock-heroics—until we realize its pathetically literal appropriateness to the vast graveyard Denmark has become.

The original Hamlet was a man who saw, too clearly, all the aspects of his situation; Laforgue's is a Hamlet who sees too clearly all the aspects of the myth which he dramatizes. He suggests that a lesser lucidity, a surrender to instinct and the unconscious, might be the cure for Hamletism:

> *Dans les Jardins*
> *De nos instincts,*
> *Allons cueillir*
> *De quoi guérir.*

[In the Gardens / Of our instincts / Let us go gather / Something to cure us] (p. 43). It is impossible for a Hamlet to follow this advice; he understands all, even that "Ma rare faculté d'assimilation / Contrariera le cours de ma vocation" [My rare faculty of assimilation / Will thwart the course of my vocation] (p. 50). A Hamlet who refers to his "scruples of existence" is disarming: while acting his role, he sees himself in the light of three centuries of criticism. The charge of solipsism that can be brought against the inhabitants of Axël's castle does not apply here.

As used by Laforgue, or by his personage, irony and comedy are, then, modes of apprehending what is, in a kaleidoscopic light. The devices may create the pose of moral and psychological realism when we are fully aware that Laforgue's allegiance is not to such realism; irony then becomes a means to indirect statement which increases, rather than "undercuts," the felt pathos, as in the closing judgment of this *Moralité*: "Et tout rentra dans l'ordre. Un Hamlet de moins, la race n'en est pas perdue, qu'on se le dise!" [And everything returned to order. A Hamlet the less, the race isn't lost: indeed!] (p. 72). Or, irony can be complexly applied to the stage properties of Hamletism, as when Laforgue apostrophizes, "Pauvre chambre tiraillée ainsi au sein d'un inguérissable, d'un insolvable automne!" [Poor room thus battered in the midst of an incurable, insolvent autumn!] (p. 21), where, despite the ridicule, a sense of this immense *ennui* remains with the reader. These are examples of a stylistic lucidity which enables Laforgue to examine all Hamlets, Shakespearean, Romantic, Decadent, and to encompass that which is mythic in the figure.

In each of Laforgue's *Moralités*, the style is adapted to the myth recreated. In *Persée et Andromède*—possibly the most successful of them all—a simple, childlike, lyric prose is created to maintain an attitude of amused sympathy toward Andromeda passing through puberty to her introduction to love. Laforgue captures all the comedy and pathos of Andromeda's insecurity and mystification before Perseus: "miraculeux et plein de chic, Persée approche, les ailes de son hippogriffe battent plus lentement;—et plus il approche, plus Andromède se sent provinciale, et ne sait que faire de ses bras tout charmants" [miraculous and

full of chic, Perseus approaches, the wings of his hippogriff beat slower—and the closer he comes, the more
Andromeda feels herself provincial, and doesn't know
what to do with her ever-so-charming arms] (p. 237).
Such a style, apposite to this fairytale, would be inap-
propriate to the essential mythic sense of *Hamlet*, for
the essence of Hamlet is contradiction, self-ridicule,
cabotinage, metaphysical bombast, agony, and poetic
creation. Laforgue's is a style truly intimate, even in
its most *cocasse* moments, with its subject matter.

His subject matter, in the largest consideration, is
myth, defined as that which is most essential and
most persistently compelling in a personage and a
story. The monologue of Hamlet, acted in the sole
theatre of our mind, finds in Laforgue its most exciting expositor, and his *Moralité* remains fresh where
Axël and even the tantalizing "Igitur"—which were
certainly intended to attain the status of myth—remain limited by their *fin de siècle* air. Paul Claudel
remarked that Hamlet was born three centuries before
his time; his appropriation by Decadent writers was
inevitable. Claudel understood that *Axël* and "Igitur"
represented the crisis of nineteenth-century metaphysics, the finest and last flowering of a Decadent monologue without future.[14] Similarly, Max Jacob claimed
that the nineteenth century invented the cult of genius and elected Hamlet its representative. He saw himself and his contemporaries as working to strip the
black tights off this figure, an attempt ultimately successful, since "the World War dehamletized avant-
garde literature." [15]

For by the time Valéry's intellectual Hamlet had
ended his soliloquy over the ideological skulls crushed
at Verdun and the Marne, the School of Paris was at
its most active, exploring primitivism and myth
within modernism. In a sense, the sophisticated juve-

nility of the douanier Rousseau is a counterpart to Laforgue's style in the *Moralités*, and Jacob's clowns and Apollinaire's Tiresias have the same mythic resonance as Laforgue's Hamlet. For the Axëls and Igiturs, the rest was silence; the theatre of the first half of the twentieth century was to develop more under the influence of *Ubu Roi*. The circus succeeded the theatre of the mind, and the terrain explored by Laforgue was fully exploited: irony and clowning were used to arrive at the mythic. That Laforgue's monologue already partook of the circus was to grant it a future denied to those other Decadent works which deployed a greater abstraction of metaphysics, but less self-criticism, a single rather than a multiple vision. Hamlet, superseded, came to be regarded as the symbol and myth of an age; yet Laforgue's Prince, because his original embodiment was inclusive and mythic, transcends the age.

The Place of Laforgue
in Ezra Pound's Literary Criticism

N. Christoph de Nagy

Ezra Pound, over several decades, both made use of Laforguian procedures and formulated criticisms of Laforgue; however, this recurrent preoccupation has been somewhat eclipsed by T. S. Eliot's relationship with the French poet. This is not merely due to a difference in fame, in particular to the much greater diffusion of Eliot's criticism and, complementarily, to the peripheral position Pound held for several decades, but also to the intensity and exclusiveness of the impact that Laforgue had on Eliot's beginnings as a poet. "Prufrock" and several other early poems written in a Laforguian key, as well as critical utterances following upon them, were in great part responsible for the increasing familiarity of the Anglo-American reading public with the name of Laforgue as the poet who enabled Eliot to carry out his poetic innovation and reinstate a "sane" poetic tradition. And since Eliot composed these early Laforguian poems prior to, and in complete independence of, the Imagist experimenting that took place in London in 1912 and 1913, it is quite possible—as in fact has often been done—to date the very birth of modern Anglo-American poetry from "Prufrock" and its companion-pieces.

In Pound's development as a poet there has at no time existed a single influence as exclusive and dominating as Laforgue's on the young Eliot. The aesthetic conception underlying Pound's very early poetry, of the so-called "Pre-Imagist Stage" (up to 1912), makes it the poet's task to find his place in the tradition by systematically experimenting with all the major existing verse forms. As one of Pound's first critical articles puts it, "the artist should master all known forms and systems of metric." [1] The first volumes of poetry, corresponding to the "Prufrock" poems, were written in accordance with this principle, but conditioned by the limitations of Pound's knowledge of poetry. They give, apart from numerous experiments with Provençal and early Italian verse forms, which, however, very significantly, are as a rule clothed in the "poetic" language of the late nineteenth century, mainly a rather complete inventory of the modes of English poetry from 1850 to 1910. Those of French poetry since the Renaissance are conspicuously absent.

The Pound of 1910 was not capable of making a decisive step beyond the state of English poetry of 1910, and that this state corresponded to a dead end, in fact to a *non essere*, will hardly be contradicted. Consequently, although the pre-Imagist poetry contains remarkable elements of lasting value, among others a new literary genre, the "persona," as a whole it was felt to be a dead end by the author himself, who gradually rejected two-thirds of the early poems. In a sense, Pound stood after the publication of his fifth volume (*Canzoni*, 1911) where Eliot had stood before the appearance of his first Laforguian poem in the *Harvard Advocate*. Now Pound, too, began looking for a tradition in another country or another century, that is, he had to enlarge the tradition already built up, according to the law that Remy de Gourmont had formulated and convincingly illustrated: "Quand il se fait un changement dans la littérature d'un pays, la cause en est toujours extérieure." [2] In the case of both Pound and Eliot the "other country" was first of all France, and, as far as France was concerned, the "other century" the second half of the nineteenth.

Pound's realization of the necessity for "making new" his own poetry was accompanied by, and in fact subordinated to, his desire and determination to reform Anglo-American poetry completely. Pound the critic was, after 1912, born out of this complex situation, with a number of periodicals like the London *Egoist* or *Poetry* in Chicago serving as vehicles for diffusion of his critical ideas. While there is hardly any criticism accompanying the very early poetry (two articles in 1911), the number of articles published within a year reaches one hundred and two in 1918.[3] After 1920, when Pound had loosened to some extent his links with contemporary literature and was concentrating on the *Cantos*, his critical output dropped suddenly. Thus his entire criticism, in which French poetry of the second half of the nineteenth century holds such an important position, was engendered merely as a means to an end. Moreover, it was closely and intricately interwoven with his own poetic development and that of his contemporaries. It appears, therefore, that a few words at this point about the character and method of Pound's criticism might not be superfluous.

The genesis of Pound's criticism as a means to an end is in keeping with the conception of the critic Pound has always had and repeatedly formulated. Criticism, he says in essence, should merely exist as *ancilla*, with the sole legitimate function of assisting the poet before the composition of poetry and the subsequent diffusion of poetry. Once these goals are attained, it has nothing further to say: "Let it stand that the function of criticism is to efface itself when it has established its dissociations."[4] Pound would probably be anything but offended if, unlike T. S. Eliot himself, one went—in ignorance—so far as to "limit" the importance of his criticism to having made him, in Eliot's words, "more responsible for the twentieth-century revolution in poetry than any other individual." [5]

Pound's conception of criticism and the motivation behind his own critical activity find their correlative in the method he adopts. This is adumbrated in an essay on Henry James, published in the same year—1918—as a translation from Laforgue and an essay about him: "Honest criticism, as I conceive it, cannot get much further than saying to one's reader exactly what one would say to a friend who approaches one's bookshelf asking: 'What the deuce shall I read?' " [6] Consequently, Pound, refraining from enunciation of critical principles unaccompanied by examples, places emphasis on concrete elements, either primarily on quotation or primarily on reference, dividing thereby the majority of his critical articles into two main groups: one containing extensive, semi-scholarly studies, such as "Early Translators of Homer" or "Notes on Elizabethan Classicists," studies of poets or literary periods unknown or imperfectly known and therefore abounding in quotations; the other containing articles expounding Pound's poetics by formulating a limited number of principles, but mainly by often unaccompanied reference to individual poets whose work forms good poetry as Pound understands it. This "Ars Poetica by Reference" implies a comparison, and its method is further developed by Pound in criticizing individual poets: they are evaluated primarily not on the basis of conceptualized qualities but in terms of their resemblances to certain other poets. The various uses to which Pound's basic method is put are well illustrated by his articles on Laforgue.

It is evident from the above that Pound, although not able to dispense with them altogether, is trying to avoid the use of concepts. The conceptualized quality covers but little of what he expects his readers to extract from a poet, and since the essential quality cannot be conceptualized Pound sought and found a different critical method. Instead of employing concepts Pound as often as possible presents an idea through a number of facts—in the context of literary criticism, through quotation and reference. This method of literary criticism, for which Pound is indebted as he says to his encounter early in 1914 with Ernest Fenellosa's essay "The Chinese Written Character as Medium for Poetry," was given the name "ideogrammic" by Pound himself. It is the method of *Ta Hio*, and is characterized by Pound in a note to his translation of this basic book of Confucian philosophy as "the Chinese or ideographic manner / which explains / not by abstraction but by citing "concrete instances." [7]

A criticism as "utilitarian" as Pound's is obviously conditioned to a great extent by the kind of writing against which it reacts and the kind of errors it seeks to eliminate. Consequently, the question suggests itself, particularly when dealing with Pound's criticism of French poets: How much of this criticism is meant to have, or can have, any significance apart from its actual impact on the literary production? Now, on the one hand, surprising as this may seem, Pound proved by his repeated republishing of many of his early articles as well as in other ways that he considered the basic elements of his criticism, despite its "utilitarian" origin, to possess permanent value. Moreover, his criticism, unlike his meandering pre-*Cantos* poetry, shows remarkable consistency as regards both the critical principles and the ideographic references between his firm establishing of his poetics in 1912–14 and the "codification" of his critical ideas in *How to Read* at the end of the twenties. For T. S. Eliot, whose authority there is more than one reason to accept in this case, the fact that Pound's criticism served as a potent medicine in a localized case—and brought about the rebirth of Anglo-American poetry in the second decade of the century—far from diminishing its value, enhances its claim to permanence. Pound's basic consistency as a critic obviously does not preclude, particularly where his championing of French poetry was concerned, certain poets from being overpraised because they provided an antidote for prevalent literary ills. As a matter of fact, in the reprint of the extensive "Study of French Poets" (1918) in *Make It New* (1934), Pound deemed it necessary to "apologize" for his erstwhile admiration for the early Francis Jammes, whose unadorned language he had expected at the time of Imagism and immediately afterwards to be helpful in freeing English poetry from the "poetic" jargon of the nineteenth century. Consequently, one must distinguish between the permanent French components of Pound's ideogram of good writing—chiefly Villon, Gautier, Flaubert, Corbière, Rimbaud, and Laforgue—and several of Pound's contemporaries whose impact appeared desirable only during a certain period. The members of the first group are, together with a number of non-French poets, those who provide Pound with the critical standards required for his comparative critical method.

A glance at the names of Villon, Gautier, Corbière, Rimbaud, and Laforgue shows clearly that in this domain as elsewhere Pound was not afraid of linking conflicting currents. Gautier in particular, as the poet of *Emaux et Camées*—and for Pound he is exclusively the poet of *Emaux et Camées*—appears to be the antipode of the other four. *Emaux et Camées,* constantly referred to during and after the Imagist campaign in 1910, had an important function as a model, since it comes very near to embodying the Imagist ideal of "dry, hard, concise," primarily pictorial poetry, with "use no superfluous word" as the central demand. However, far from looking upon this work of Gautier merely as a therapy in a localized case, Pound retains, and reiterates the expression of, his full admiration and as late as 1928 writes: "Gautier j'ai étudié et je le révère." [8] *Emaux et Camées,* unique as an attempt at equating craftsmanship with poetry, must be, for Pound, part of a valid tradition.

One does not learn without surprise that for Pound Laforgue "marks the next phase after Gautier in French poetry," [9] a statement the negative consequences of which T. S. Eliot makes a point of emphasizing in the otherwise enthusiastic introduction to the *Literary Essays*: viz., "he ignores Mallarmé, he is uninterested in Baudelaire." [10] If the Gautier of *Emaux et Camées* corresponded to the Imagist ideal, it is understandable that Baudelaire, Verlaine, and Mallarmé could not aspire to this position; in a sense, Imagism with its insistence on the sharp, single image was at the antipode of Symbolism with its insistence on the complex and purposefully vague image. Baudelaire and Verlaine, being fairly well known in England and America, needed no propaganda, and, moreover, Pound did not think them "useful" for the "making new" of Anglo-American poetry: "neither of them is the least use, pedagogically, I mean. They beget imitation and one can learn nothing from them." [11] As for Mallarmé, his name is hardly even mentioned. It appears that for Pound the pedagogical "uselessness" of these poets between 1912 and 1914 was not counterbalanced by interest in their poetry.

Despite his enthusiasm for Rimbaud, Laforgue is the only Symbolist to whom Pound devoted close critical attention.

While most of the major Symbolists are conspicuously absent from Pound's tradition, the name of Gustave Flaubert recurs with astonishing frequency, more than once coupled with Laforgue's. For Pound, who with his admiration for the French novelist stands in line of succession to Ford Madox Ford, Flaubert is as important a component of the ideogram of good writing as Gautier; both proved to be indispensable support for the central endeavor of Pound's critical activity, namely that of dethroning the Romantic conception of poetry and reinstating poetry as an *art*—with all the ensuing consequences. In this respect as in many others, England and America were lagging behind France, and to meet the demands put upon him by poetry conceived as an *art* the English or American poet, according to Pound, could not do without the help of Flaubert. Moreover, it was one of Pound's aims, often published, that the reform initiated by Imagism should raise Anglo-American poetry to the artistic level of French prose—the prose of Flaubert. Yet the desirability of Flaubert's impact on poetry was not limited to the period 1910–20, for even in *How to Read* Pound maintains: "I believe no man can now write really good verse unless he knows Stendhal and Flaubert." [12] Pound's references to Flaubert imply among other things that a careful study of Flaubert's impersonal art, and in particular of the details of his craftsmanship and all it involves, would perforce make it impossible for any poet to write "Old Vicarage Granchester," neo-Swinburniana or quite generally the diffuse and verbose kind of poetry against which Pound was campaigning after 1912, but which has been produced in all ages.

Gautier and Flaubert—*Parnasse et Réalisme*—were Pound's most frequently referred-to favorites when, after his meeting with T. S. Eliot in September, 1914, and most probably in connection with study of the latter's poems, he made the acquaintance of Laforgue's poetry; that is, about three years after he had first read the other modern French poets and popularized some of them. After 1915 references to Laforgue become fairly numerous in his letters, and in the fall of 1917 he published his extensive critical estimate in Harriet Monroe's *Poetry* under the title "Irony, Laforgue and Some Satire." The following year saw publication of his "Study of French Modern Poets," the first essay being devoted to Laforgue.

The essay in *Poetry* appeared in the year that witnessed publication in book form of the "Prufrock" poems by the still unknown T. S. Eliot, and it is worth noting that while Eliot was saturated with Laforgue quite a number of years before Pound got to know the latter, it is Pound who can claim priority in having popularized Laforgue.

The position Pound found himself in towards 1917, after his Imagism had brought about the first stage of the poetic revolution—that is, to put it in terms of French poetry, before he added the world of *L'Imitation de Notre-Dame la Lune* to that of *Emaux et Camées*—is vividly and convincingly characterized by Warren Ramsey, whose article "Pound, Laforgue and Dramatic Structure" makes it perfectly superfluous for the present writer to deal with the important problem of the actual impact of Laforgue on Pound: "Structurally speaking, the Imagist poem tends to be the elaboration of a single visual image, or else it places end to end a series of such images, in a compound but not a complex relation. The ambitious poets among the Imagists—Pound in so far as he was an Imagist—sensed limitations of method, straitness of viewpoint within their program, and began to cast about for techniques which would permit them to respond to complex realities in a complex way. It was at about this point of creative dissatisfaction that Pound began to read Laforgue." [13]

In Pound's criticism of Laforgue, born of such creative dissatisfaction, the different variants of his critical method are well illustrated. The essay on Laforgue in the long "Study in French Poets" stands as an extreme case of that variant of the "ideogrammic" method which presents an author through quotations with very little critical text. In *How to Read*, as well as in a number of other general critical articles, we find a more restricted application of this method, namely, mere references to poets whom Pound considers essential, coupled with brief remarks as to the qualities they embody. Finally, Pound's most important study of Laforgue, the essay "Irony, Laforgue and Some Satire," belongs to those essays that, developing the above method further, evaluate an individual poet primarily by comparison with "essential" writers. However, it must be mentioned that precisely in the course of evaluating Laforgue's poetry, Pound, not always given to consistency, appears to complement his "ideogrammic" method by frequent use of a term of his own coinage, a concept that has a significant position in his criticism.

Pound's principal essay on Laforgue, packed with critical information, establishes links with permanent ideas and figures of his criticism. It also proves, through what it says and what it leaves unsaid, to be singularly illuminating as regards Pound's development around 1917. To begin with what is left unsaid, it surprises one that in an essay on Laforgue, who to put it with all desirable caution, was the first modern poet of importance in Europe to make extensive use of *vers libre*, no remark should be made by a successful champion of this form regarding his metrical experiments. The reason for this may well be, in tune with the pragmatic character of Pound's criticism, that in 1917 the problem of free verse did not strike Pound as *actuel*. At that time the joint decision of Pound and Eliot to return to the greater rigor of rhyme and regular strophe after, in Pound's words, "the dilution of *vers libre*, Amygism, Lee Masterism, general floppiness had gone too far," was in the making.[14]

If Laforgue's metrical experiments do not draw forth any comments, neither does, whether in approbation or disapprobation, his revolutionary use of colloquial speech as such, though Pound, once more following in the footsteps of Ford Madox Ford, has all along been preoccupied by the question of poetic language, and has always stipulated the use of the language of the time. Again it appears that after the "sins" of "Amygism" (the dilution of Imagism by Amy Lowell), "Lee Masterism," and so forth, the above problem was not *actuel*; or it may simply have been crowded out of the essay by Pound's preoccupation with qualities that he found nowhere but in Laforgue.

Basic and dominating among these—and stressed by the title—is the ironic quality of Laforgue's verse. This, nothing sensational in itself, furnishes another indication that Pound is moving in the direction of an intellectually more exacting poetry. Irony, always resulting from the contact of two contrasting elements, requires a different kind of thinking from the poet than that required for the composition of Pound's favorite "Carmen est maigre," and it forces the reader to redoubled attention, as it were. In the words of

Pound: "The ironist is one who suggests that the reader should think and this process being unnatural to the majority of mankind the way of the ironical is beset with snares and furze-bushes." [15] The chief characteristics of the essay are, first, the emphasis placed upon Laforgue's work as primarily satire of his predecessors (and not as an extremely complex expression of his personality) and, second, the equal attention given to Laforgue's prose and poetry. The key sentence of the essay reads: "Laforgue was a purge and a critic." [16] And applying his comparative critical method he likens Laforgue to Flaubert—a great compliment, coming from Pound—in particular to the Flaubert of *Bouvard et Pécuchet*, a work for which Pound always professed immense admiration (not widely shared) and which he used as a basis for his evaluation of *Ulysses*: "He has done, sketchily and brilliantly, for French literature a work not imcomparable to what Flaubert was doing for 'France' in *Bouvard et Pécuchet*, if one may compare the flight of the butterfly with the progress of an ox, both proceeding toward the same point of the compass." [17] Thus, Laforgue's work represents an implicit satirical criticism of the French literature of the first three-fourths of the nineteenth century. The concrete instance of Laforgue's work performing this critical task mentioned by Pound and elaborated on concerns, somewhat surprisingly, Flaubert himself: "He laughed out the errors of Flaubert, i.e., the clogging and cumbrous historical detail. He left *Coeur Simple* [sic], *L'Education, Madame Bovary, Bouvard*. His, Laforgue's, 'Salomé' makes game of the rest." [18] The *Moralités légendaires* as such—their "philosophy," and the like—are not even mentioned; Pound merely catches on "Salomé" parodying Flaubert, which he considers a stylistic purge. This purge concerns a writer who was, and remained, one of Pound's deities;

and more generally, it concerns the impersonal and exacting art of realism, which, virtually non-existent in England, had again and again been held up as a model in Pound's criticism. Although Pound's words merely condemn the laboriously exact historical reconstruction, this latter presupposes the search for the *mot juste* as such, a parody of which is, consequently, included in Laforgue's "Salomé." And it is this parody on Flaubert's realism that Pound works into a free translation, which he entitles "Our Tetrarchal Précieuse (A Divagation from Jules Laforgue)," first published in 1918 and subsequently reprinted in *Pavannes and Divisions*. For Pound, "Laforgue implies definitely that certain things in prose were at an end," and his translation of this *conte* rather than another seems to indicate that Laforgue helped Pound to obtain a fuller, better differentiated view—including the limitations—of Flaubert and "realism" in general. In fact, when the new prose did appear—*Ulysses*—Pound was among the very first to recognize its significance. As for Laforgue, if he was purge and critic of nineteenth-century French literature, he proved to be purge and critic of Pound's critical ideas as well.

In evaluating Laforgue's poetry, his major achievement, after all, Pound attempts to employ his usual comparative method. What happens, however, is that he sees himself reduced to a series of negative comparisons: "This is not the strident and satiric voice of Corbière . . . , it is not Tailhade . . . , it is not Georges Fourest . . ."—statements of a not too illuminating character. The truth is that Pound's comparative method, which would not only recognize links between Corbière and Villon but would also establish unexpected ones, between Rimbaud and Catullus, for example, simply fails when it comes to Laforgue. The reason for such negative comparisons is explained, over a decade later, in *How to Read*: "Laforgue is not like any preceding poet." [19] He virtually alone represents one of the three kinds of poetry into which, deviating from or perhaps rather complementing his "ideogrammic" method, Pound, for the first time in 1918, divides all poetry: *logopoeia*. The other two are *melopoeia* and *phanopoeia*, for the last of which Pound in 1918 characteristically still uses the term "imagism." In the summary of Pound's critical ideas, *How to Read*, which occasioned the controversy with F. R. Leavis (who qualified Pound as "amateur of abstractions") [20] the three categories occupy a central position, and the French poets are discussed in terms of them.

> There are three kinds of poetry:
>
> MELOPOEIA, wherein the words are charged, over and above their plain meaning, with some musical property, which directs the bearing and trend of the meaning.
>
> PHANOPOEIA, which is a casting of images upon the visual imagination.
>
> LOGOPOEIA, 'the dance of the intellect among words,' that is to say, it employs words not only for their direct meaning, but it takes account in a special way of habits of usage, of the context we *expect* to find with the word, its usual concomitants, of its known acceptances, and of ironical play.[21]

About the practitioners of *logopoeia* Pound says: "Unless I am right in discovering *logopoeia* in Propertius . . . , we must almost say that Laforgue invented *logopoeia*, observing that there had been a very limited range of *logopoeia* in all satire, and that Heine occasionally employs something like it together with a dash of bitters, such as can (though he may not have known it) be found in a few verses of Dorset and Rochester. At any rate Laforgue found or refound logopoeia." [22]

To what extent is this conception of Laforgue's

poetry as "dance of the intellect among words" borne out by the facts? That Laforgue's originality is to a great extent lexicographic, that he delights in playing with words, is revealed at the first glance by many signs—even before the meaning of a poem is fully grasped—quite particularly by the frequent occurrence in his poetry of so-called "contaminations" like "éléphantaisiste," "sexciproque" or "ennuiversel." A decomposition of these contaminations, on the other hand, points to the most characteristic trait of Laforgue's language as a whole, his eclecticism as to the sources from which his vocabulary is derived. While the most conspicuous and unusual of these sources is the scientific one—François Ruchon found in *Complaintes* alone "lymphatique," "corrosif," "madrépore," "albumine," "mucus," "chrysalide," "réflexe," "syncope," "plasma," "métamorphose," "lexicon"—it is in fact possible to distinguish five main sources, the other four bringing forth proverbial expressions and "clichés," popular and especially *argotique* expressions, literary allusions, philosophic and religious terms.[23] The mere presence within a poem of more than one of these groups would result in an unusually complex vocabulary. The presence of all of them in Laforgue's poetry after *Le Sanglot de la terre* justifies Pound's contention that "the intelligence of Laforgue ran through the whole gamut of his time." [24] All this, however, is not *logopoeia* yet, even though it is hard to imagine a poetry based on *logopoeia* that would dispose solely of the vocabulary of Racine. Laforgue's eclectic vocabulary as such appears merely as an indication that he had not suffered from what T. S. Eliot was to call, in words frequently quoted, "the dissociation of sensibilities." We can only speak of *logopoeia* when the words constituting this tremendously varied vocabulary begin to take one another's places, when they crop up in unexpected contexts. In fact, the different parts of Pound's definition of *logopoeia* can be brought to a common denominator which is *meaning affected by context*, and *logopoeia* can be defined as a principle of poetry that induces the constant and purposeful alteration of the meaning of words by placing them in contexts other than those of traditional usage. Whereas *phanopoeia* uses the pictorial and *melopoeia* the musical quality of words and word combinations, *logopoeia* can be said to exist by virtue of the semantic properties of words.

It does not follow from Pound's definition—or from the deductions one can make—that *logopoeia* is necessarily an instrument of irony. It is true though that the precursors of Laforgue in the use of *logopoeia* were satiric poets; however, because of its short history, no definite conclusions can be drawn. With Laforgue, at any rate, *logopoeia* is completely in the service of his irony, which in turn depends exclusively on manipulation of words.

The basic procedure of this Laforguian *logopoeia*— following from the above definition—either involves a word or expression belonging by nature to one of the five groups of specifically Laforguian vocabulary or one that remains within the framework of the traditional vocabulary. In the first case the typically Laforguian expression is at times slightly changed, lifted out of its habitual context by being attached to a "normal" word. Through the contact both expressions lose some of their original meaning, and a new ironical meaning is born:

> *Astre sans coeur et sans reproche*
>
> *A travers maman, amour tout d'albumine*
>
> *Faites que ce crachoir s'éloigne un peu de moi!* [25]

In the second case, less often met with, the words themselves have nothing extraordinary about them, and the irony depends exclusively on their being lifted out of their usual context:

> *La terre est orpheline*
> *Aux ciels, parmi les séminaires des Routines.*[26]

The alteration of meaning is not always easily perceptible. Thus in "*Introïbo,* voici l'Epoux!"[27] "époux" would be perfectly in tune with the context of the poem, "Complainte des noces de Pierrot," but "Epoux"—the divine "Husband" of the mystics—changes the relationship between meaning and context entirely. In certain cases the meaning of a word is further multiplied by a kind of bifurcation of the original meaning, or of that created by the unusual context, or both. In "J'entends battre mon Sacré-Coeur,"[28] we have on the one hand "Sacré-Coeur" as signifying the Sacred Heart itself or as signifying the Church building (and "I hear" as suggesting the Church bells); on the other hand, applied to the poet, the word may retain its exalted meaning but stand for a personal "coeur sacré," and finally we get to the fourth, the ironical meaning of "sacré coeur." We have in fact not merely the dance but the somersault of the intellect among words.

Pound is not the sort of critic who would invent a term like *logopoeia* without wanting to make use of it for his own poetry. The first step in this direction appears to have been Pound's attempt to translate a poem of Laforgue showing a particularly thorough application of the principle of *logopoeia.* Now Pound says that "*logopoeia* does not translate. . . . but having determined the original author's state of mind you may or may not be able to find a derivative or an equivalent."[29] Pound in his translation of "Pierrots (Scène courte mais typique)" is definitely seeking an equivalent. His translation somehow lacks the colorful vivacity of the original, but it lays the foundation

of a new poetic style on which Pound was to erect
important structures. His translation, particularly its
rhyme and vocabulary, is the most important evidence
of Laforgue's decisive impact on "Hugh Selwyn
Mauberley."

In Pound's conception Laforgue is both an end and
a beginning, and his own relationship with the French
poet can be evaluated in terms of this dual position.
For Pound, Laforgue was the "end of a period" because his satirical purge indicated that certain things
in nineteenth-century literature could not develop further.[30] The concrete instance of Laforgue fulfilling
this critical function that Pound mentions—and illustrates with his own translation—concerns Flaubert's art, and Laforgue's parody appears to have been
a significant factor in the clarification of Pound's view
of prose. However, in Pound's conception Laforgue is
also a beginning, for he founded a kind of poetry that
Pound considers important enough to constitute one
of the three basic categories into which he divides all
poetry. This contention is borne out by the fact that
the young T. S. Eliot, whose poetry and criticism
turned out to be very much of a "beginning" for the
literature of our century, chose Laforgue as a starting-
point. It is in the poetry of Laforgue and of the
English Metaphysicals that the young T. S. Eliot took
refuge from what he later called "the dissociation of
sensibility," that is, very broadly speaking, the divorce between thinking and the composition of poetry, and Laforgue as well as the English Metaphysicals became important pillars of his tradition. In the
words of Pound, "T. S. Eliot has gone on with
[logopoeia]." [31]

For Pound himself, the meeting with Laforgue
means a beginning. Since he had not read the French
poets at the outset of his career, this is a "new start."

It is Laforgue who enables Pound, chiefly by means of the principle baptized *"logopoeia"* to evolve a new poetry that can deal with complexities, particularly those of our contemporary world, in an adequate manner. Pound's "Hugh Selwyn Mauberley" is the most immediately recognizable result of this meeting, but the *Cantos* themselves are not unaffected by Laforgue.

The fact that Pound and Eliot tried their hand at *logopoeia* usually in combination with the Laforguian ironical attitude must not lead to the conclusion that *logopoeia* necessarily calls for irony. Laforgue's *logopoeia* seems to have initiated quite generally a verbal art characterized by enhanced consciousness of the semantic malleability of words. Such awareness was fundamental to a literature that refuses to withdraw from an age as complex as ours. It is in this sense that Laforgue's *logopoeia* proved to be of assistance to Pound just as during the Imagist period Gautier's phanopoeia had.

Pound derived benefit from the acquaintance with Laforgue for his own development as a poet as well as for the clarification of his critical ideas; and as an act of considerable objective value he popularized the essential characteristics of Laforgue's poetry at a time when he was the most influential literary pedagogue and critic in the Anglo-American world. In these achievements, his criticism still plays the part of *ancilla* in the service of the writing and diffusion of poetry. Yet in his criticism of Laforgue as elsewhere Pound goes beyond his own conception of the exclusively pragmatic function of criticism insofar as he evaluates Laforgue's importance by identifying an essential principle of his poetry. *Logopoeia*, brought into existence by Laforgue, is seen as opening up new roads for poetry altogether.

Jules Laforgue and Samuel Beckett:
A Rapprochement

Erika Ostrovsky

> In my end is my beginning.
> ("East Coker")

The words of T. S. Eliot might have been written as an epitaph for Jules Laforgue, so well do they sum up the destiny, the continuing heritage, the growing strength of Laforgue's poetic vision. The end of his work has truly been the beginning for a line of writing which is an integral part of the contemporary literary scene. Laforgue is so peculiarly modern that he plays the interesting dual role of predecessor and contemporary of today's writers. He is a paradoxical and many-sided artist and it is not surprising that his heritage should be as multiform as his own work. The lighter and more facetious side of Laforgue's writing, the *non sequitur* capers of his heroes, his delight in incongruity, in the confounding of reason, seriousness, and logic, have been reaffirmed by a line of authors from Apollinaire and Cocteau to the Surrealists, and finally emerge in such recent works as those of Ionesco.[1] But there is another, darker side of Laforgue's poetic universe which is perhaps even more essential to his vision. It is one characterized by a deep awareness of the terror, loneliness, and abjectness of human existence, the grotesqueness of man's strivings, and the paradoxical dignity which he retains despite all this. Such a vision has reappeared along the path traced by an-other group of writers who are engaged upon a jour-ney farther into the kind of night which Laforgue had already entered. We can include Céline, the early Sartre, and finally Beckett, among the voyagers.[2]

In many ways, Samuel Beckett seems to be one of Laforgue's closest spiritual kin among the contempo-raries. One may hesitate to assume direct influence of Laforgue on Beckett, although this is by no means an impossibility. One may point to a line which leads from Laforgue to T. S. Eliot to Beckett,[3] or from Laforgue to Joyce to Beckett.[4] One may analyze the similarities to be found in the work of Laforgue and Beckett and establish the possibility of a *rapproche-ment* between them, as this essay will attempt to do. More important than any of these theories, however, is the fact that Laforgue has directly or indirectly contributed to the formation of those who have come after him. He has helped to create the literary milieu in which we are living today; his view of existence is so much one of *this* century that he cannot help being currently influential.

A certain aspect of Laforgue's poetic vision seems to reach its culminating point in the work of Samuel Beckett. Fundamentally it is the view of man as both a ridiculous and a tragic figure, and of his life's quest as both a defeat and an ultimate affirmation. Such a relatedness between two writers seems to be much more one of kindred sensibility than a simple case of literary discipleship. If Beckett has gone on where Laforgue left off, he has both retained and developed an entire literary inheritance which the latter has left to our century.

At times, however, it seems that the link between the two writers is almost continuous. This becomes apparent in the case of two works, "Hamlet, ou les suites de la piété filiale," of Jules Laforgue,[5] and *Fin de partie* of Samuel Beckett,[6] which present such surprising parallels as to oblige us to link them together or at least to consider their relationship. If one puts Laforgue's tale and Beckett's play side by side, one cannot help but be struck by certain resemblances. One notices first of all, a similarity of setting: the tower in which Hamlet lives reminds us of the room in which *Fin de partie* takes its course. It is almost as if the first were seen again in a mirror which had the power of reflecting and accentuating all its properties. Both rooms are bathed in a grayish, leaden light. Each contains two windows, one facing the static sea, the other the land. Hamlet's tower stands on a stagnant body of water where debris is deposited; Hamm's room is surrounded by a world in the state of stagnation and decay. In the tower, paintings line the walls; in the room described by Beckett there is only one painting, with its face turned to the wall. A cupboard figures prominently in both settings: Hamlet's cupboard to which he alone possesses the key, designed to safeguard his life from the attacks of enemies; Hamm's cupboard, for which only he knows the combination, containing the poison by which his life can be ended.[7] Hamlet keeps two waxen figurines concealed in an alcove, white effigies of the corrupt king and queen, reminders of the past, of filial duty and of vengeance. In *Fin de partie*, two white-faced puppets appear from their ashcan hiding places, reminders of the past and objects of vengeance, an old king and queen of the chess game which takes its course there. In Hamlet's tower the season is perpetual autumn (even in July), the sky remains unchanging; in Hamm's room there are no seasons at all, no changes in the weather or in the state of things. While in Laforgue's tale, time is abolished by means of anach-

ronisms, in *Fin de partie,* time is abolished *per se.*
Both rooms are "dens," "retreats," or "shelters," in
the sense that Beckett uses the word: they are removed from the world or opposed to it, centers of
refuge as well as of stagnation. The quality of removal
and stagnation is partial in Laforgue, complete in
Beckett.

The two principal actors, Hamlet and Hamm, are
strikingly similar, even disregarding the obvious resemblance of their names. Both are outcasts or voluntary exiles, both "end" at the close of the work, Hamlet in venturing out of the tower, Hamm by remaining
in the room. While both characters have obvious ties
with Shakespeare's Hamlet, both involve fusions of a
number of mythical, historical, or literary figures.
Thus, Laforgue's Hamlet is compounded of Shakespeare's, of Pierrot, and of Nero, of Saxo Grammaticus' Amleth,[8] of Mallarmé's Igitur,[9] and even of a bit
of the court fool (since he turns out to be, in the tale,
the brother of poor Yorick by a gypsy mother).
Hamm, it has been suggested, resembles both Shakespeare's Hamlet and a ham actor;[10] he reminds us of
Noah isolated in his ark, as well as of Noah's son
Ham, the hateful, who, ironically enough, was
charged in the Bible with re-peopling the world after
the flood; he also shows resemblances to Christ, to
Lear, and to the wounded Fisher King.

Hamlet and Hamm are both writers. In general,
they write badly, wish desperately to be heard, use art
as a palliative for their essential despair. Both are complex creatures, not only because of the fusions suggested above, but also because they show evidences of
a dual nature: they are both hero and anti-hero, equally
legendary and *"terre à terre,"* tragic and trivial, humor-
ous and despairing, timeless and limited to the narrow
confines of the moment. Their actions, which vacillate

continuously, show this dualism, but it becomes most pronounced in their speech. The latter varies between eloquence, mock-eloquence, and slang, poetic utterance, and crudity or banality. It vacillates, contradicts itself, is purposely incongruous or antithetical, yet manages by these very oppositions to achieve its great power and unity of expression.

Hamlet and Hamm seem to be heroes of the absolute as well as of the absurd. In each of these realms the ordinary human value scheme is meaningless or to be rejected or, as Hamlet says, "Tout est permis." [11] In both instances, filial piety is abandoned or ridiculed, cruelty and pity alternate almost indiscriminately; love, friendship, or communication between human beings, have become difficult in Laforgue's tale, impossible in the play by Beckett. In both instances the microcosm is pitted against the macrocosm. In Laforgue's work, the battle between the two still rages, but Beckett has pretty well annihilated the macrocosm, and the microcosm is in the process of "ending."

It can be seen that in general Beckett has gone further along the path indicated in Laforgue's tale. This is true for the setting, in which the painting faces the wall instead of the spectator, the cupboard which contains the means of ending life instead of preserving it; it is equally true for the fusions involved in creating the principal character of each work. The figures of which Hamlet is composed are not quite as tragic in nature as those which are suggested by Hamm. Human experience is limited in Laforgue's tale but reaches its utmost reduction in Beckett's play. In the same manner, Hamm's circumnavigation is in some ways the further development of Hamlet's journey. Hamlet's was a voyage out, ending in death. Hamm's journey proceeds in an inward direction, in a series of ever-narrowing circles which lead to a dead center; the shroud becomes the still point at which all movement ceases. Hamm, "the castled king," [12] is the extension of Hamlet, the castled prince, who leaves the protection of his tower. One and the other, however, is checkmated at the end of the game he has played.

Although the parallels in the two works are often quite close, it would be absurd to presume that any meaningful *rapprochement* of Laforgue and Beckett could be made on the basis of these alone. The affinities of the two authors far exceed such narrow boundaries and affirm themselves in related stylistic traits, principal themes, and in a basically similar orientation toward existence. It is within the larger framework of the writers' work as a whole that their kinship becomes most apparent.

If we consider first some of the stylistic traits of Laforgue and Beckett, we already find a fair number of similarities. Conversational tone has an important place in the work of both.[13] Laforgue and Beckett use it even in the treatment of intensely emotional subject matter. In both cases, conversational tone frequently seems to be a manifestation of irony in the sense of unexpectedness, since low-toned language is used to depict a situation of deep emotional impact. It might also be considered a method of emphasizing paradox and incongruity, or simply of shocking the reader into a more intense awareness. Parody and learned allusion used with ironic intent are favorite techniques of both writers. Even if one does not go as far as stating that all of Beckett's plays are a "parody of theatre," [14] or claiming that large parts of Laforgue's writings are parodic in intent, examples of both the devices mentioned are fairly frequent in the works of both authors. The most clear-cut use of parody and learned allusion with ironic intent can be found in Lucky's speech in *Waiting for Godot* and in Laforgue's tale, "Salomé."

Both writers relish incongruity of dialogue, plays on words, and puns. Although Beckett does not go as far as one of his characters, who claims, parodying Genesis, that "in the beginning was the pun," [15] he nevertheless makes it one of his favorite devices for producing humor. Laforgue's use of anachronism is somewhat related, for it is a kind of play on dates, a device which produces, among other things, an intellectual chuckle in the reader. The use of varying tones which oppose each other, the lofty versus the colloquial, the intellectual versus the commonplace, the pathetic versus the mocking, has already been referred to in the discussion of Hamlet and Hamm and their speech pattern. One might add that the humor of both writers is often based on a similar kind of juxtaposition: a combining of laughter and terror into a *humour noir*, a paradoxical mixture which accentuates as well as softens despair. In Laforgue's work, this type of humor appears only at times,[16] and is often replaced by a lighter and more facetious merriment. In Beckett's writing it is almost the only kind of laughter we are permitted.

Interior monologue, the kind of stream-of-consciousness composition which Laforgue had begun to experiment with in his last works,[17] reappears in such early works of Beckett as the *Nouvelles et textes pour rien*. Of course, the technique is much more fully developed in Beckett, since at least fifty years and such writers as James Joyce and Virginia Woolf have intervened, but the link with Laforgue is there, even if indirectly.

The use of varying "voices," each one speaking from a different level of experience, a region of the human mind or a point in time, is one of Laforgue's most fascinating and novel stylistic devices. We witness its presence in the work of Beckett, also, especially in his play of 1958, *Krapp's Last Tape*, where the voices of the past and present, of dream and crude reality, the voices of memory and forgetfulness, the loud voice of youth and the almost silent one of old age, all mingle, are juxtaposed, predominate in turn, fuse into a new whole, very much the way they do in Laforgue's most successful creations of this kind.[18]

In general, one might say that both Laforgue's and Beckett's style reflect an attitude of constant opposition: that of feeling tones, of language, of "voices." It seems based on the authors' concern with antithetical attitudes and is perfectly suited to the portrayal of such attitudes. While in Laforgue's case, the style suits his basic statement of the paradoxical nature of existence and the many-sidedness of human experience, in Beckett it reveals the fundamentally static quality of despair, the uselessness of a move in any direction, or the meaninglessness of any statement. Whereas antithesis leads to the assertion of a complex unity in Laforgue, for Beckett it serves to emphasize the disjointed and futile motions of beings who are poised on the brink of nothingness. While the first underlines the complexity of existence, the latter summarizes its lack of meaning and therefore its lack of cohesion. While all statements are meaningful to Laforgue, all are almost equally meaningless for Beckett. Antithesis, or moves in various directions, serve to emphasize the continuous movement and lack of fixity which characterize human experience, in the work of Laforgue. For Beckett, one move tends to be as empty as another, and the futile motions in varying directions serve only to strengthen the awareness of fixity. However, while Laforgue and Beckett seem to diverge in regard to the use which they make of antithesis, the basic concept of opposition or dualism is present in both.

A similar concern with antithesis prevails in other than stylistic areas as well. If we look at the protagonists of both authors—one hesitates to call them heroes, though they so clearly manifest a heroic as well as an anti-heroic nature—we find that they resemble each other as a result of this very duality. They are often banal, ridiculous, grotesque, or *"terre à terre,"* yet retain a certain tragic dignity, a legendary or mythic splendor, despite these failings. This is perhaps most clearly seen in the case of Hamlet and Hamm discussed earlier. However, it is apparent in all the protagonists of both authors. The creatures of Laforgue are more graceful, to be sure, and less hideous than those of Beckett, but one suspects them to be of the same parentage. The figures who appear in Beckett could be the relatives of those of Laforgue, a few generations removed, and their traits exaggerated as a result of further breeding within the same family. Most of them are nomads: the Pierrots, *saltimbanques*, gypsies, and sons of gypsies, that Laforgue describes, the buffoons, clowns, mimes, and wanderers of all sorts who appear in Beckett. Their natural habitat seems to be that of the circus, the music hall, the *Funambules*, or the Punch and Judy show. But their life's journey takes place on the outskirts of the crowd, away from human existence in general, and leads them toward a realm which might be called that of the absolute. If such an existence is characterized by "a mingling of metaphysics and music hall," [19] where Beckett's characters are concerned, in Laforgue it resembles a mixture of metaphysics and the antics of the circus clown. In the work of both writers we are dealing with figures who move on many planes at once, complex, paradoxical creatures, difficult to portray or summarize. Not only do the protagonists exist on various time levels, since they assume mythic or immortal proportions and yet are confined to the narrow limits of the present moment, but they also show such antitheses in their character traits that we cannot define them except by a series of paradoxes. They are tragic buffoons, lofty and trite, poetic and crude, laughable and terrifying, revolting and intensely moving. There is a difference of degree concerning these traits in the work of the two authors. Laforgue's protagonists are comparable to the figures which appear in his drawings: if they are skeletons, they nevertheless assume amusing poses while dancing and never fail to appear wearing the top hat of the dandy. If we wished to arrive at an imaginary drawing of Beckett's characters, we would have to resort to an exchange of hats (an old vaudeville trick). His protagonists would then appear as skeletons in grotesquely amusing poses, and wear the bowler hat of the *clochard*, that image of the outcast, of human débris, who appears so frequently in Beckett's writings. If such a procedure is a somewhat facetious one, the comparison nevertheless seems to summarize the resemblances and differences that exist in the heroes of both writers.

It is in their principal themes that Laforgue and Beckett show the closest spiritual kinship. Beckett's preoccupation with disease, impotence, emotional, intellectual, and physical paralysis, is so well known and so constant throughout his work as to need no further elaboration. It reaches its high point, however, in the description of the Lynch family, whose five generations and twenty-eight members suffer from every disease known to man.[20] But Laforgue is almost equally concerned with such matters. We find constant references to disease in people and even objects, to human fragility, the destruction of the body, impotence or

sterility, in his writings. And if both the diseases and
remedies are those of the last century, if we find tuber-
culosis and heart ailments, *tisanes* and cough medi-
cines in Laforgue, their presence is almost as pronounced as that of amputation, inflammation of the
prostate, catheters, tonics, tranquilizers, and morphia,
in the work of Beckett. The deterioration and decay
of man which Laforgue had already described in his
poems,[21] is left to Beckett to explore in all its most
appalling forms. But there is also another kind of
destruction, that of "primary human experiences," [22]
which Laforgue had depicted in his frequent negation
of friendship, love, communication, reproduction, and
the sense of belonging. All these human experiences
have been even further eliminated in the work of
Beckett. This is perhaps most clearly shown in *Fin de
partie*, where warmth and contact between human
beings have become quite impossible, and in *Krapp's
Last Tape*, where only the mechanical voice of the
tape recorder persists as a reminder of human communication in the far-off past.

For Laforgue, reality, or the *"ici-bas,"* and all its
adherents, are vulgar, hateful, to be ridiculed or escaped from. Beckett has gone further in that he denies
the very reality of the real,[23] and annihilates the outer
world which is its embodiment. This annihilation
seems to appear in all his novels, from *Murphy* to *The
Unnamable*, and also becomes apparent in the stage
settings of his major plays, which grow less and less
representative of the outside world as we progress
from *Waiting for Godot* to *Krapp's Last Tape*. Even
language itself, as a possible manifestation of reality,
has been eliminated by the mimes which Beckett has
come to be so much concerned with. In the case of
both writers we find a fundamental tendency to sacrifice the everyday, the contingent, to the absolute or

the essential, with a stripping-away of the first in order to arrive at the second.

This brings us to what is perhaps the most interesting point of encounter between Beckett and Laforgue. For the movement away from the contingent, the recurrent "quest of the absolute," [24] in which their heroes are engaged, leads them to a realm which is startlingly similar. It matters little that Laforgue gives this domain the title of moon, aquarium, tower, or palace, or that Beckett refers to it as a shelter, a den, or finally gives it no name at all (in *The Unnamable*, of course). The names are deceptive, for the region is always the same. It seems to be located deep within the mind of the individual and reached through a "contraction of the spirit, a descent" [25] into the self. Such a journey leads into those *"fonds silencieux pour lesquels c'est toujours l'éternité,"* [26] which Laforgue has described, or that darkest region of the mind of which Beckett has said that it was a "matrix of surds," [27] where *"abreuvé de noir et de calme, au fond du jour profond,"* [28] the individual is "more and more and more in the dark, in the will-lessness, a mote in its absolute freedom." [29] It is also the place where, as Laforgue states it, one abandons oneself *"sans volonté et sans force dans la vie inconsciente. . . ."* [30]

The Unconscious, for Laforgue, is generally synonymous with Eduard von Hartmann's *"das Unbewusste,"* which is both a Nirvana beyond the strivings of the will or the squalor of existence, and a life force. In Beckett it may resemble the race-unconscious of the Jungians, where such archetypal figures as that of the "mother-destroyer" in *Molloy* [31] have their reign, but it does not differ very much from the region which Laforgue had referred to as the *"Saint-Sépulcre maternel."* [32] Whatever the psychological concept which underlies the idea of such a place, it is defined by both authors in a curiously similar manner. Its topography and the conditions which exist there are almost identical: fixity, calm, and silence prevail. The light is vague or failing, the senses are restricted or dead, a physical and spiritual numbness has taken over. Reason is obliterated, the will is weakening, all the functions of the human creature are slowly stripped away. This is most clearly shown in the various descriptions of the aquarium in the work of Laforgue, and in Beckett's portrayal of the region in which the action (or lack of action) of *The Unnamable* takes place. However, we also find many other descriptions of similar realms in the work of both authors.

Impotence and sterility are the rule of this land. In Laforgue's kingdom of the absolute, there is no fecundation, and even the fruit is deprived of seeds.[33] In Beckett's *Fin de partie*, even the lowly flea is not permitted to copulate, for all of human misery might be recaptured by this action.[34] Being born into the world is considered a curse, or at least an imposition; fecundity is both incongruous and dangerous in the realm of the absolute. Both Hamlet and Hamm express this. Hamm damns his father for being an "accursed progenitor," [35] and frantically counsels Clov to kill the flea who might re-establish the order of the world. Hamlet emphasizes the fact that he *"ne fut pas facile à attirer dans ce monde d'ici-bas,"* [36] and had to be born by means of force (that is, by Caesarian section). In the regions of the absolute there can be no movement, no fertility, for these are attributes of the world of the *"ici-bas"* and must be eliminated in the former to distinguish and cut it off from the latter. The danger of re-establishing the order of the outer world is emphasized by the protagonist of *The Unnamable*, who says of the realm in which he vegetates that "here all change would be fatal and land me back, there and then, in all the fun of the fair." [37] The ironic use of the word "fun" and the pejorative reference to the world as a "fair," remind one of a similar attitude of Laforgue, who often speaks disdainfully of the everyday world as "*la foire*," or "*la kermesse*," and contrasts it with the changeless calm which prevails in the regions of the absolute. In order to avoid movement, change, or fertility in the latter, sexlessness and even castration [38] are emphasized by Laforgue. In Beckett, castration or amputation becomes so drastic that the creature who figures in *The Unnamable* is deprived of all senses, features, and appendages, and is left with nothing but empty eyesockets that stare into darkness [39] and a voice to tell his tale. All is "*figé*" in Laforgue's world of the absolute, or "corpsed," to use Beckett's stronger adjective.

However, the absolute of Beckett and Laforgue is much more complex than these first observations would indicate. It is a paradoxical place which is both a haven and a site of annihilation, a refuge and the final *cul de sac*, a womb and a necropolis, a protection and a mortal danger, a realm of deliverance and paralysis. This becomes quite clear in many of Laforgue's works, but is expressed most vividly in the poem, "*Climat, faune et flore de la Lune*" (*O.c., I.,* 262). It is equally apparent in the many passages in Beckett's writings which refer to this realm. Murphy speaks of the "absolute freedom which reigns there," [40] Malone mentions the deliverance he feels because "all was streaming and emptying away. . . . until finally nothing remained," [41] and "the black joy of the solitary way in helplessness and will-lessness," [42] he experiences. And yet the same realm is also the hell of fixity that is shown in *Fin de partie*, in *Malone Dies*, and in *The Unnamable*, where the annihilation that has been sought for becomes a terrifying reality. Malone had affirmed that "nothing is more real than nothingness,"[43] but when this nothingness threatens to become a reality, it is quite dreadful to behold or experience. Hamm cries out to his father, to Clov, to inanimate objects, even, before entering into the final silence. All of Laforgue's heroes who have searched for the absolute and been destroyed by it, express their terror when annihilation is imminent. Hamlet, Salomé, and the Syrinx, utter a quite human cry in the face of destruction. Even when the heroes are not destroyed, the absolute nevertheless threatens them with a death-in-life existence, with a dreadful fixity which Laforgue has compared to that of *un miroir mort* in the poem, *"Climat, faune et flore de la Lune."*

Finally, this domain of stagnation, dissolution, and annihilation, where the individual and all his human faculties are destroyed, is, strangely enough, also the place where they reach their greatest expression. For both Laforgue and Beckett see it as the domain of art and the artist. Laforgue states this quite frequently in his work;[44] all of Beckett's protagonists who exist in this realm are writers, or at least tellers of tales. Malone guards his notebook and pencil stub long after all his possessions and most of his faculties have disappeared. Hamm works and reworks his story until the last moments of *Fin de partie*. Although the protagonist of *The Unnamable* is finally possessed of nothing but his voice, he continues to tell his tale.[45]

The key to this paradox might be found in the conception of the artist which Laforgue and Beckett share. Both seem to feel that the artist must strive for the annihilation of consciousness, yet retain a shadow of this very consciousness to be able to tell his tale. Laforgue is quite explicit on this. He describes it as a state of *"annihilation de la conscience, sauf un soup-çon de persistance de quoi jouir de son annihilation."* [46] A similar condition is portrayed in *The Unnamable* where the protagonist yearns "to enter living into the silence so as to be able to enjoy it." [47] The artist is thus seen as a three-sided figure: he is the victim and the executioner of annihilation as well as the *deus ex machina* who saves him from being utterly destroyed by it. And all the realms of silence, whether they are that of the moon, the aquarium, the white island, or Hamlet's tower in Laforgue, or that of Murphy's garret, the padded cell, Mahood's vase, Hamm's room, or Worms' final subterranean haunt in Beckett—all do have one exit and one exit only: the very thin path of the artist's voice which cannot be silent, is clamoring to be heard, not yet to be quite annihilated. When all seems on the point of ending, *"seuls les mots rompent le silence, tout le reste s'est tu."* [48] And we might conclude by saying, in the spirit of Laforgue and Beckett, that for both writers, in spite of everything, before the final silence, triumphing over annihilation, "In the end was the Word."

Phryne, or More Than One Right Word
Warren Ramsey

*Quand est-ce que nous nous montrerons adéquats à la va-
leur des phénomènes et vivrons-nous justes de ton?—Jules
Laforgue, quoted by his brother Adrien* [1]

Laforgue's work was done in a day of marked single-
mindedness. He turned up at the edge of the literary
scene when the doctrine of Art for Art's sake had
given rise to works that most of us would be prepared
to recognize as the most "perfect" of modern times.
The notion of art as complete unto itself, having no
end beyond itself, had a poetic parallel: the idea of
the absolute line, verse, word. Aesthetic and poetic
absolutes had, in short, rushed into the vacancy left by
the crumbling of other absolutes. Those—like Mallarmé—most given to noting the decline of other systems of belief were also those who insisted on the
quasi-magical properties of the unique poetic word. It
would be ungrateful to dispute an assumption that
gave us some of the purest, most crystalline, of all
poetry and prose.

It was a distinctive quality of Jules Laforgue that he
acknowledged no aesthetic absolute and looked toward no unique solution of any poetic problem. He
revised, mainly for the better, like other poets. We
have "Fabius Cunctator," as he nicknamed his publisher, partly to thank for the fact that *Les Complaintes* has so much precocious authority. Léon Van-

ier's Hamlet-like delays held up this first book for
fifteen months, allowing a rapidly developing author
time for second and third thoughts. But no one who
has sought to follow the workings of this poetic mind,
in particular the shaping of his last poems and his
verse play out of a discarded collection, can fail to
appreciate a difference between Laforgue and his contemporaries. He envisions alternatives. He is capable
of finishing the "same" poem in different, equally
effective ways.

Derniers Vers has its considerable merits. And it is
tempting to see in this free verse of the last phase a
culminating accomplishment, an instrument peculiarly responsive to complexities of the human mind
being assessed at the time by, say, Charles Henry, the
Tainean psychologist who was Laforgue's friend. Set a
passage from *Derniers Vers* beside the earlier one
from which it was rehandled, however, and it is not
easy to say which is better.

"Figurez-vous un peu!" [2] (from *Des Fleurs de
Bonne Volonté*) is all in stalwart alexandrines, with
pauses and tonic accents at points well calculated to
heighten the effect:

> *Oh! qu'une, d'elle-même, un beau soir, sût venir,*
> *Ne voyant que boire à Mes Lèvres! ou mourir . . .*
>
> *Je m'enlève rien que d'y penser! Quel baptême*
> *De gloire intrinsèque, attirer un "Je vous aime"!*
>
> *L'attirer à travers la société, de loin,*
> *Comme l'aimant la foudre; un', deux! ni plus, ni*
> *moins . . .*

Turned into free verse, rechristened "Les Amours"
and given an ironically impressive epigraph from Petrarch,[3] this keeps the declamatory opening couplet,
with its breathless first line, then becomes:

> *Oh! Baptême!*
> *Oh! baptême de ma Raison d'être!*
> *Faire naître un "Je t'aime!"*
> *Et qu'il vienne à travers les hommes et les dieux,*[4]
> *Sous ma fenêtre,*
> *Baissant les yeux!*

Substantives receive much greater emphasis, syntactical connectives much less. Couplets give way to more fluid rhythmic units that cast the substantives into relief. Here the theme, a characteristic one, is the meeting of a young man whose innocence has become slightly suspect with a young lady whose guilelessness remains beyond reproach. Quotation marks set off the first of these voices:

> *"Pour moi, tu n'es pas comme les autres hommes,*
> *"Ils sont ces messieurs, toi tu viens des cieux.*
> *"Ta bouche me fait baisser les yeux,*
> *"Et ton port me transporte*
> *"Et je m'en découvre des trésors!*
> *"Et je sais parfaitement que ma destinée se borne*
> *"(Oh! j'y suis déjà bien habituée!)*
> *"A te suivre jusqu'à ce que tu retournes,*
> *"Et alors t'exprimer comment tu es."*

Varying line lengths allow the independent logic of the verse without overflow:

> *Ainsi, elle viendrait, évadée, demi-morte,*
> *Se rouler sur le paillasson que j'ai mis à cet effet*
>   *devant ma porte.*
> *Ainsi, elle viendrait à Moi avec des yeux absolu-*
>   *ment fous,*
> *Et elle me suivrait avec ses yeux-là partout,*
>   *partout!*

The expansive lines are commensurate with the fervor, and details have greater immediacy. It is a question, however, whether wit did not benefit from brevity, from absence of quotation marks and from the solemn march of the couplets.

"Solo de Lune" is interestingly compounded from the taut quatrains of "Arabesques de Malheur" (vv. 8–16, 32–35, 42–45, 47–50, 103–5). The first stanza of the earlier poem becomes, with an added and distancing syllable, this second strophe of "Solo de Lune":

> *Nous nous aimions comme deux fous,*
> *On s'est quitté sans en parler,*
> *Un spleen me tenait exilé,*
> *Et ce spleen me venait de tout. Bon.*

Another quatrain is turned into five—more flexible— lines. And the new version has its full complement of dark satanic mills and workaday words of a kind then unexpected in poetry, missing from the earlier draft:

> *On a dépassé les filatures, les scieries,*
> *Plus que les bornes kilométriques,*
> *De petits nuages d'un rose de confiserie,*
> *Cependant qu'un fin croissant de lune se lève,*
> *O route de rêve, ô nulle musique . . .*

Here the poet discovers liquid beauties in the "r's" and "l's" of "filatures" and "scieries." No parts of the poem are more interesting, however, than those most delicately, almost imperceptibly retouched. An earlier quatrain runs:

> *Des ans vont passer là-dessus;*
> *On durcira chacun pour soi;*
> *Et bien souvent, et je m'y vois,*
> *On ragera: "Si j'avais su! . . ."* [5]

The first line is unchanged in *Derniers Vers*. The others become:

> *On s'endurcira chacun pour soi,*
> *Et bien souvent et déjà je m'y vois,*
> *On se dira: "Si j'avais su . . ."*

Certainly the first of these lines has become more musical, in the Verlainean sense, for having acquired a ninth syllable. And the second line, something more than ten syllables in length because of the variable "bien," has much of the movement of Laforgue's free verse at its best. It suggests the following, where the third line sings like no ordinary alexandrine, because of the placing of the caesura and the mute "e" and nazalized vowel of "légendes" just before it:

> Ah! ce n'est plus l'automne alors,
> Ce n'est plus l'exil.
> C'est la douceur des légendes, de l'âge d'or,
> Des légendes des Antigones,
> Douceur qui fait qu'on se demande:
> "Quand donc cela se passait-il?"

This is similarly developed from briefer, tighter form ("Dimanches," XXX, *Des Fleurs de Bonne Volonté*). With its second and fourth lines in five and nine syllables respectively, such a passage goes far toward realizing the ruling musical objective of the day. Meanwhile the earlier version remains rich with the traditional music of shorter and more regular lines.

Another "Dimanches" (XLIV, *Des Fleurs de Bonne Volonté*) brings its contribution to this same "Légende," and the free verse growing out of it succeeds, on the whole, despite a certain drift toward exuberance. But Laforgue was more effective in the first draft of another passage, deservedly well known. The first two lines anticipate the note which was to be prolonged in Eliot's "Portrait of a Lady."

> (—Voici qu'elle m'honore de ses confidences;
> J'en souffre plus qu'elle ne pense!)

> Chère perdue, comment votre esprit éclairé,
> Et ce stylet d'acier de vos regards bleuâtres

N'ont-ils pas su percer à jour la mise en frais
De cet économique et passager bellâtre? —
—Il vint le premier; j'étais seule devant l'âtre . . .

> *Hier l'orchestre attaqua*
> *Sa dernière polka.*[6]

> *Oh! l'automne, l'automne!*
>   *Les casinos*
>   *Qu'on abandonne*
> *Remisent leurs pianos! . . .*

> *Phrases, verroteries,*
> *Caillots de souvenirs.*
> *Oh! comme elle est amaigrie!*
> *Que vais-je devenir! . . .*

Adieu! les files d'ifs dans les grisailles
Ont l'air de pleureuses de funérailles
Sous l'antan noir qui veut que tout s'en aille.

> *Assez, assez,*
> *C'est toi qui as commencé.*

With further spacing out of voices and an **added**
touch in lines eight and nine, this becomes:

> *Enfin; voici qu'elle m'honore de ses confidences.*
> *J'en souffre plus qu'elle ne pense.*

> *—"Mais, chère perdue, comment votre esprit éclairé*
> *"Et le stylet d'acier de vos yeux infaillibles,*
> *"N'ont-ils pas su percer à jour la mise en frais*
> *"De cet économique et passager bellâtre?"*

> *—"Il vint le premier; j'étais seule près de l'âtre;*
> *"Son cheval attaché à la grille*
> *"Hennissait en désespéré . . .*
> *—"C'est touchant (pauvre fille)*

"*Et puis après?*
"*Oh! regardez, là-bas, cet épilogue couleur de
   couchant;*
"*Et puis, vrai,*
"*Remarquez que dès l'automne, l'automne!*
"*Les casinos,*
"*Qu'on abandonne*
"*Remisent leur piano;*
"*Hier l'orchestre attaqua*
"*Sa dernière polka,*
"*Hier, la dernière fanfare*
"*Sanglotait vers les gares . . .*"

(*Oh! comme elle est maigrie!*
Que va-t-elle devenir?
Durcissez, durcissez,
Vous, caillots de souvenir!) [7]

One would have to quote fifteen more lines of "Légende" to demonstrate fully how images and traits of
the earlier poem have been diluted. The underlying
error is that a lyric interlude, an incipient choral comment, has been woven into the remarks of an ironic-
pathetic young man whom the author wants us to
believe in, to accept as a flesh-and-blood figure, coming and going in the society of his time. Added quotation marks fail to conceal a new confusion of voices, a
blurring of edges. There are also minor losses in immediacy, as when "bleuâtres" becomes "infaillibles."

No such softening of contours can be detected in
Le Concile féerique, the little verse play assembled
out of five earlier poems. It struck Jean-Aubry as surprising that Laforgue should have used materials on
hand, keeping them virtually intact. Given the poet's
manner of working, however, there is nothing remarkable in such procedure. His earliest *complaintes* had
projected, separated out voices. Sometimes, as in "Petites Misères de juillet," one of the poems assimilated
into *Le Concile féerique*, this was done with the aid

of quotation marks. More often, the spacing is established by *les blancs*, those white margins of passage
and poem and page which Laforgue, along with other
poets of his generation, used to such good effect. In
either case, poems and passages here fall naturally into
parts for Gentleman, Lady, Chorus, and Echo. Over
all is the Starry Night, seen as a guaranty of an eternal
rhythm, if not necessarily of moral law or of an Eternal Spectator.

The Gentleman is duly meditative:

> *O Loi du rythme sans appel,*
> *Le moindre astre te certifie*
> *Par son humble chorégraphie!*
> *Mais, nul Spectateur éternel . . .*
> *Ah! la terre humanitaire*
> *N'en est pas moins terre-à-terre!*
> *Au contraire.*[8]

The Lady is close kin to that "eternal humorist"
whose characteristics Eliot was to suggest in "Conversation Galante" and other poems. She embodies an
image of womankind developed by nineteenth-century idealists:

> *Si mon air vous dit quelque chose,*
> *Vous auriez tort de vous gêner;*
> *Je ne la fais pas à la pose.*
> *Je suis la femme, on me connaît.*[9]

She is known, this incarnation of the life force, for her
protests against nervous excitement:

> *Oh! ces nuits sur les toits!*
> *Je finirai bien par y prendre le froid . . .*[10]

And for expressions of good will:

> *Ah! vas-y; je n'ai plus rien à prendre à cet'heur';*
> *La Terre est en plein air, et ma vie est gâchée;*
> *Ne songe qu'à la Nuit, je ne suis point fâchée.*[11]

The chorus offers advice that may have entered into the background of Apollinaire's *Alcools*:

> *Les vignes de vos nerfs bourdonnent d'alcools*
> *   noirs,*
> *Enfants!* [12] *ensanglantez la terre, ce pressoir*
> *Sans planteur de justice!*

There is also choral counsel of a different stamp:

> *Hé! pas choisi* [13]
> *D'y naître, et hommes;*
> *Mais nous y sommes,*
> *Tenons-nous-y!*

So swift and colloquial is the observation that one can overlook its direness, its similarity to those made by choruses in antiquity.

Arrangement of main parts is at least as important here as details. There is a tendency, quite the opposite of that ordinarily discerned in Laforgue's verse, toward tauter organization. Passages are symmetrically balanced. Patterns of force become more pronounced. Alexandrines are retained but octosyllabics are more strategically placed. A crisp economy, a sharpness of detail, contrast forcefully with nonchalant attitudes expressed.

As quotations from *Derniers Vers* attest, one of the persistent motifs is that of a *persona*, identified as Lohengrin, Pierrot, someone else, or simply unnamed, who pulls the bride up short. The young man of "L'Impossible," inclined to lonely meditation beneath the stars, continues "à la seule clarté des étoiles" in "Nuit d'Août." The lady's attitude, in that posthumously published fragment, makes him think of Phèdre's tormented outcry, "Que ces vains ornements, que ces voiles me pèsent!" A little later the lady murmurs, "Tes boutons de manchettes m'ont fait mal." The young man's contemplative spirit may not have been victorious here. But in "Lohengrin, Fils de Parsifal" it is, and Lohengrin declaims:

> *Il était un roi de Thulé*
> *Qui, jusques à la mort fidèle,*
> *N'aima qu'un cygne aux blanches ailes,*
> *Voilier des lacs immaculés.*
>
> *Quand la mort vint . . .*[14]

This is, incidentally, much closer to Gérard de Nerval's version of the German poem than to Laforgue's own "Complainte du roi de Thulé."

Imagery of whiteness is even more concentrated in the final pages of "Lohengrin" than in "Complainte du roi de Thulé" or in the poems dealing with Laforgue's wan-faced Pierrot. Recalling that Lohengrin had first complimented her for her swanlike neck, Elsa "fait la morte . . . mais non, sa main insiste sur un point . . .

> "—*Comment appelez-vous ça?*
> "—*Je ne sais; la pomme d'Adam.*
> "—*Vous dites?*
> "—*La pomme d'Adam.*
> "—*Et ça ne vous rappelle rien?*
> "—*Ma foi non.*
> "—*Et v . . . va donc! Moi ça me rappelle les plus mauvais jours de notre histoire!*"

Lohengrin's desperately clutched pillow, "white and pure like a swan," is in fact metamorphosed to the swan that had brought the knight to Elsa. As it spirals upward toward the Milky Way and mirrorlike glaciers beyond, the reader realizes that there is less difference than at first appeared between this morality and "Nuit d'août," where he is told outright that the hero meets his end. The same symbolic pattern is to be found in many a poem of Laforgue's middle period, where Pierrot meets his own kind of Columbine, and where remarks of a general kind, out of keeping with either character, are interlarded.

Laforgue was living in a cottage on the grounds of Babelsberg Castle, looking out over the park, where kingfishers dived for little silver fish, and reflecting on the *struggle for life* (as he wrote in English), when the idea for *Pierrot fumiste* came to him. As published in fragmentary form a decade later, the first scene is, as first conceived, "sur l'escalier de la Madeleine, la sortie du mariage de Pierrot." Even as the wedding party emerges, undertakers are arriving, and workmen are busy nailing up black draperies bearing the initials C. P., those of Pierrot's bride, Colombinette, as he is first to point out. There is a prosperous beggar to whom Pierrot grandly gives "un faux louis, un louis faux, c'est tout ce qu'il loui faut"—the donor says, but perhaps the coin is genuine. We further meet an outraged suisse; the bride's undaunted mother; a coachman who manages to drag Pierrot out of the funeral coach where he has taken refuge, and installs him in the wedding carriage with Colombinette. Escaping through the opposite door, Pierrot is finally apprehended in the flower market, inquiring everywhere for *rosa sempervirens funulariflera*, a plant apparently unknown except to him and Linnaeus. Failing to find it, he buys a bunch of violets for Madame Ventre, the news-vendor. Not till an alcoholic addresses him as a capitalist does Pierrot make his way thoughtfully back to the carriage, ask Colombinette if she is firmly in possession of her capital, and take his place, though he darts out again to order the wedding party off to Cytherea, and there are still further vacillations.

The second act has scenes at midnight, at 3:20 A.M., at an unspecified hour when Pierrot recites Boi-

leau's "Ode sur la Prise de Namur" against the weakness of the flesh, and at 8 A.M., when, with a grace
worthy of Marcel Marceau, he brings Colombinette
her coffee. A main Laforguian motif is presented with
a certain balletlike simplification here. In projected
final scenes, Pierrot, faced with the growing disquie-
tude of Colombinette, her mother and her friends,
amply makes up for his shortcomings and procrastina-
tion before skipping off to Cairo. But Laforgue only
sketched out this atypical climax and conclusion; it is
as though he did not really want to finish his play in
this fashion. A main Laforguian motif is left in high
relief. And it is a sign of precocious maturity that it is
presented in this comic mode, with humor that is
broad without ever lapsing into the merely grotesque, as well as in the more lyric idiom of the poems
and tales. The tables are turned. Pierrot or Pedrolino,
languishing with unrequited affection ever since the
early days of the *commedia dell'arte*, makes Columbine languish instead. These reversed attitudes run
underneath nearly all of Laforgue's poems, tales, and
dramatic efforts, to be reversed themselves only in the
last-written of his stories, "Pan et la Syrinx ou
l'invention de la flute à sept tuyaux." There the characters, no longer those of the *commedia dell'arte*, or
those of the *commedia* artfully up-ended, take on
some of the roundness of the believable. This is done
with no inhibition of the language. Here are a few
lines spoken by the Emancipated Feminine—it was,
after all, a period marked by dramatic exits from dolls'
houses, by doors vengefully slammed:

> "*Je ne suis pas un petit paon,*
> "*Je ne suis pas une poupée!*
> "*Je me suis tout échappée*
> "*Pour venir échouer sur le coeur du grand Pan!*
> "*Oh! je suis pure comme une tulipe*

"*Et vierge de toutes espèces de principes!*
"*Avril! avril!*
"*Mon bonheur ne tient qu'à un fil!*"

Quotation marks were apparently called for because the faun's fanciful, Laforguian nymph is speaking. Before the sunlit pastoral is over, most of the main lines of the myth have been restored. The Equivocal Masculine lets himself go in verses like these:

Oh! viens-tu, tout à l'heure?
Où aller te chercher,
Ma fragile Psyché
Que chaque instant déflore
Loin de mes bras prospères?

Oh! ce sera tant toi!
Ingénieusement je t'emmènerai
Au plus profond des bois,
Là où il fait le plus frais;
Et puis tu pourras t'étirer sur le gazon,
Après tant d'après-midi virginales,
Et t'abandonner à la bonne saison
Dans l'assourdissement des cigales . . .

But of course the long chase ends quite differently—with a choral maxim. It cannot really be Syrinx who says, "Vous voyez bien, vous-même; il n'y a que l'art; l'art c'est le désir perpetué." It can hardly be she who whispers over the water at the moment when the seven-pipe flute is wrought: "Vite, vite, c'est son âme qui passe en ces roseaux que tu tiens!"

In lyric, dramatic and narrative forms, in language increasingly responsive to shades of thought and feeling, Laforgue gives poetic voices to the men and women of his time, with contrapuntal comment on the pathetic limits set to their satisfactions.

Those who value his poetry and prose are justified in seeking its conditions if not its occasions in a more

or less systematic aesthetics, in an underlying philosophy of composition. His theory of a Hartmannian
Unconscious blowing where it listeth, discovering and
imposing forms, served at least to justify, in a young
poet fighting for life against deterministic paralysis, a
native need for freedom. It encountered a natural
spontaneity, rationalized a sense of the variety of creative experience, the richness of its manifestations. It
confirmed the interest of the temporary, of the human
figure decked out in the strange fashions of a given
moment in time as well as of the human figure nude,
universal, timeless. It allowed Laforgue the young art
critic to dwell on the possibilities of polychromatic
sculpture, to remember that those Greek figures so
much admired by Renan and Taine had once been
colored with golds and reds and blues. That commentary on Impressionist paintings which runs through
his writings, and was probably indispensable to his
development as a poet, found support in this aesthetics. So did his anticipations of Futurism, willingness
to reckon with the industrial life of cities.

In its emphasis on the necessary timeliness of artistic expression, this doctrine stands revealed as the
recalcitrant offspring of Taine's, pursuing the factors
of racial strain, environment, and particularly the
most mysterious of the triad, the historical moment,
somewhat further, with a certain rebellious delicacy.
The youthful auditor at Taine's Beaux-Arts lectures
balked at the value judgments, at the comfortable
words. Art that deals with something stable and permanent is not, Laforgue tells us, inherently superior to
that which reflects the transitory; a healthy frame of
mind is not a more commendable subject than a
sickly one. Repudiating didactic content, he refuses to
judge works of art on the basis of their "beneficent"
effect. He further differs from Taine—as from Poe and

the line of poets influenced by Poe—in refusing to accept "convergence of effects" as a criterion. There is no perceptible effort toward unity of effect in his poems or prose from the *Complaintes* forward.

On the other hand, there is much deliberate under-cutting of any conceivable total effect. There are digressions, willful shifts in point of view, rapid changes of tone; despite this, a poem or story line remains readily distinguishable. Variations and var-iants are not traceable to a demiurgic Unconscious. They are simply due to fluctuations within what La-forgue calls "la pauvre créature." They are the inven-tions of an extraordinarily responsive poetic mind, working now on one of the levels of imagination, now of the level of fancy, with a swift saying and unsaying of things, a freedom of utterance, which is one, but only one, of its qualities.

Of how many Mauberleys would it have to be said that their "true Penelope was Flaubert"? Fascination with the mysteriously right word must have driven and sustained many of those who appreciated the fertility of Laforgue's mind and prolonged his work. But Laforgue had no Penelope, not even Flaubert, for all his tribute paid in honest coin of parody and satire. Not even Stendhal, though a critic of the time re-ferred to his unfinished novel (probably the one of which "Nuit d'Août" is an episode) as "du Stendhal gracieux." Revealing though it is, the formula is by no means exhaustive. No single writer can be pointed out as one to whom Laforgue returned regularly for exam-ples of excellence or for inner strength. He may have had several heroes, a whole pantheon, at once. But that is another matter. There is none of the usual monism, no consuming admiration for a single great writer.

His critical taste, in short, like his aesthetics and

poetics, took unusual account of alternatives. He was a pluralist in a day of convinced monists, a poetic skeptic during the ascendancy of a splendid *idée fixe*. Repentant schoolboy though he was, burdening his verse and prose with half-assimilated speculations that never fully jelled, he nevertheless anticipates one of the complete poets of our time, the Valéry of "Mémoires d'un poème," in whose mind the same literary subject developed in a variety of ways, who confessed to a "perverse mania for possible substitutions" and dreamed of the work that would suggest the "*possible-à-chaque-instant*" of reality, who published different versions of the same poem.

The youthful adept of the Impressionists, the aesthetician who sought to formulate the theory behind their paintings in a full-scale essay, the art critic who commented on their practice in *salons*, in numerous letters and in glittering bursts of poetic high spirits, was also in search of the literary work that would suggest the boundless possibilities rather than a unique determination of reality. He would have agreed with Valéry that the former kind of aesthetic illusion is "plus véritable" than the latter. Thus he returns us to some of the sources of Valéry's variety: among others, to a conception of the poem as something larger than its shape upon the page, an essentially oral form whose nature might be renewed by modern means of reproducing the voice. We are brought closer to some of Valéry's underlying attitudes and tentative conclusions: that the conflict between the two mighty voices, the two literatures of intellect and imagination, may not be quite hopeless, if only one is willing to believe that poetry is also a means of discovering something new about the world, a means differing in degree of intensity, but not in kind, from the more halting forms of search.

What Laforgue discovered most particularly, perhaps, in that delicate poetic language of his, alternately orotund and spare, which he compared to Phryne's *sincère nu* in that *livre de bonne foi* which his work considered as a whole approximates, was the endless and contradictory division of the so-called individual. Those deep complexities stood rather dizzyingly revealed to the nascent psychology, the visual arts and the poetic intuition of his time. Because he found the means to face, as a poet, a vision of the mind's deeper hesitations and inconsistencies, others were able to do so after him. In a time of many true believers he offered the example of a creative mind unfailingly true to itself, otherwise unconvinced.

Notes

Laforgue in America COWLEY

1. Besides Damon, Burke, Cummings, Wheelwright, and Hart Crane, some of the other poets who read Laforgue with admiration in the years around 1920 were Louise Bogan, Allen Tate, and Yvor Winters (but not Léonie Adams, who read him later).

Leah Laforgue, Her Parents and Family LEE

1. David Arkell, "Leah Laforgue," *Times Literary Supplement*, June 10, 1965, p. 480.
2. Writing to his sister Marie. *Œuvres*, V, 170.

Laforgue Among the Symbolists PEYRE

1. *Poetry: A Magazine of Verse*, IV (March 1914), 26–27.
2. This and other quotations from T. S. Eliot have been collected and intelligently utilized by Edward J. H. Greene in his *T. S. Eliot et la France*, 1951.
3. The *Derniers Vers* have been carefully edited and prefaced by Michael Collie and J. M. L'Heureux, University of Toronto Press, 1965.

Laforgue and His Time WEINSTEIN

1. Later published in book form as *Enquête sur l'évolution littéraire* (Paris: Charpentier, 1913).
2. The most frequently mentioned names in Jules Huret's index give a fair, if not altogether accurate, indication of their relative importance: Maurice Barrès (37),

Paul Bourget (26), Alphonse Daudet (22), Gustave Flaubert (28), Anatole France (26), the Goncourt brothers (40), Victor Hugo (43), Joris Karl Huysmans (27), Leconte de Lisle (22), Stéphane Mallarmé (46), Jean Moréas (59), Henri de Régnier (27), Paul Verlaine (44), Emile Zola (77).

3. Quoted in Pierre Martino, *Parnasse et symbolisme* (Paris: Armand Colin, 1925), p. 144.

4. Listed in Jacques Plowert, *Petit Glossaire pour servir à l'intelligence des auteurs décadents et symbolistes* (1888), quoted in Pierre Martino, *op. cit.*, p. 145. There is, of course, another side to this trend of verbal inventiveness, and we find it in Laforgue who coins new words by joining old ones with ironic suggestiveness (Eternullité, sangsuelle, etc.). Cf. Warren Ramsey, *Jules Laforgue and the Ironic Inheritance* (New York: Oxford University Press, 1953), pp. 137–39.

5. This is an example of "la poétique volapukiste" as found in *Lutèce* of March 3, 1886:

> *Stals vamik sola de plum*
> *Vietoms vatis de flum*
> *E faloms flamik as tum*
> *   Sagits Lofapula!*
> *On âklôdom-ôv das fel*
> *Binom logad: lino, Spel.*
> *Ekômom svidik as smel*
> *   Flolas ets lulula.*

6. Cf. the remarks of Verlaine (p. 71) and Leconte de Lisle (pp. 279, 284) in Huret, *op. cit.*

Laforgue and the Theatre   BLOCK

1. Gustave Kahn, *Symbolistes et Décadents* (Paris, 1902), p. 27.

2. Marie-Jeanne Durry, *Jules Laforgue* (Paris, 1952), p. 66.

3. Laforgue, *Œuvres complètes* (Paris, 1925), V, 146. The discovery and publication of Laforgue's letters to Paul Bourget could add much to our knowledge of the poet's aspirations as a playwright.

4. For a detailed study of the fate of Laforgue's papers, see J. S. Debauve, "A propos des manuscrits de Jules Laforgue," *Revue d'Histoire littéraire de la France,* LXIV (1964), 656–67.

5. See Gustave Kahn, "Jules Laforgue," *Les Nouvelles Littéraires,* le 29 décembre 1928, p. 7.

6. Raymond de Casteras, *Avant le Chat-Noir: Les Hydropathes,* 1878–1880 (Paris, 1945), p. 29. Also see Jules Lévy, *Les Hydropathes* (Paris, 1928).

7. For a detailed account of the poetic clubs and cabaret performers of the day, see Noël Richard, A *l'Aube du symbolisme* (Paris, 1961), pp. 9–59.

8. The relationship is indicated by Raymond de Casteras, p. 240; it may well repay detailed study.

9. *Ibid.,* p. 76.

10. *Ibid.,* p. 196.

11. Cf. Gustave Kahn, "Jules Laforgue en Allemagne," *Les Nouvelles Littéraires,* le 12 janvier 1929, p. 4.

12. Cf. Laforgue, "Théâtres" in *Œuvres complètes* (Paris, 1930), VI, 148–49.

13. *Ibid.,* VI, 243.

14. See "A Propos de Hamlet" in *Chroniques Parisiennes. Ennuis non rimés* (Paris, 1920), pp. 53–57.

15. Laforgue, *Dragées. Charles Baudelaire. Tristan Corbière* (Paris, 1921), p. 18. The entry is dated "le 31 décembre 1884."

16. *Ibid.,* p. 25. The entry is undated.

17. The text may be found in Laforgue's *Mélanges posthumes, Œuvres complètes* (Paris, 1910), III, 87–107. For the tradition underlying Laforgue's Pierrot, see A. G. Lehmann, "Pierrot and *fin de siècle*," in Ian Fletcher (ed.), *Romantic Mythologies* (London, 1967), pp. 209–23.

18. Laforgue, *Exil. Poésie. Spleen* (Paris, 1921), p. 32.

19. The play apparently was not performed. For a brief account of the collaboration of Huysmans and Hennique, see O. R. Morgan, "Huysmans, Hennique et 'Pierrot sceptique,'" *Bulletin de la Société J.-K. Huysmans,* No. 46 (1963), 102–4.

20. Laforgue, *Œuvres complètes* (Paris, 1925), IV, 67.

21. Pierre Reboul, *Laforgue* (Paris, 1960), pp. 88–89.

22. *Ibid.*, pp. 66–67. More appropriately, the play may be seen as expressing the same disgust with the sexual aspect of woman that is found in Laforgue's poems and letters. See the observations of M. Collie and J. M. L'Heureux in Laforgue, *Derniers Vers* (Toronto, 1965), p. 88.

23. *Ibid.*, p. 89.

24. Pauline Newman-Gordon views the play as "vengeance contre la femme" in *Corbière, Laforgue et Apollinaire* (Paris, 1964), p. 56; but it is difficult to take Colombinette's alleged suffering realistically. A similar anti-feminism can be seen in *Pierrot sceptique*, and was no doubt commonplace in cabaret pantomime.

25. Stéphane Mallarmé, "Notes sur le théâtre," *Revue Indépendante*, III (avril 1887), 61.

26. Laforge, *Œuvres complètes*, IV, 208.

27. *Ibid.*, IV, 215.

28. *Ibid.*, V, 16.

29. *Ibid.*, V, 44.

30. Warren Ramsey, *Jules Laforgue and the Ironic Inheritance* (New York, 1953), pp. 118–19.

31. Reboul, p. 89.

32. Cf. Michael Collie, *Laforgue* (London, 1963), p. 76.

33. For a detailed account of the transposition, see François Ruchon, *Jules Laforgue* (Genève, 1924), p. 257; also, G. Jean-Aubry in Jules Laforgue, *Poésies complètes* (Paris, 1943), II, 157.

34. Laforgue, *Lettres à un Ami* (Paris, 1941), p. 190.

35. Gustave Kahn, *Symbolistes et Décadents*, pp. 185–86.

36. See the discussion of Dorothy Knowles, *La Réaction Idéaliste au théâtre depuis 1890* (Paris, 1934), pp. 155–56.

37. William Jay Smith (ed.), *Selected Writings of Jules Laforgue* (New York, 1956), p. 80.

38. Camille Mauclair, "Le Cinquantenaire de Jules Laforgue," *Revue de Paris*, XLIV (15 juillet 1937), 349.

39. Théodore de Banville, *Poésies complètes* (Paris, 1891), III, 281–82.

40. Banville, *Critiques* (Paris, 1917), p. 267.

41. See Mallarmé, *Correspondance; 1862–1871* (Paris, 1959), p. 166.

42. *Ibid.*, p. 327, n. 1.

43. For a more detailed account, see my study, *Mallarmé and the Symbolist Drama* (Detroit, 1963), pp. 83–100.

44. Mallarmé, "Notes sur le théâtre," *Revue Indépendante*, II (janvier 1887), 55.

45. Gustave Kahn, "Un Théâtre de l'Avenir," *Revue d'Art Dramatique*, 15 (juillet–septembre 1889), 342.

46. For an excellent discussion, see Jacques Robichez, *Le Symbolisme au théâtre; Lugné-Poe et les débuts de L'Œuvre* (Paris, 1957), pp. 104–41.

47. Paul Fort, *Mes Mémoires* (Paris, 1944), p. 31.

48. Cited in Robichez, p. 113.

49. *Ibid.*, pp. 122–23. For the program, see pp. 492–95.

50. For an entertaining account of the performance of P.-N. Roinard's work, see Georges Maurevert, "Des Sons, des Goûts et des Couleurs," *Mercure de France*, 292 (le 15 juin 1939), 561–64.

51. Adolphe Retté, *Le Symbolisme* (Paris, 1903), p. 200.

52. See Adolphe Retté, "Le Concile Féerique," *Le Livre d'Art*: Programme de la Première Représentation de la Saison 1891–92, p. 3. A copy may be consulted at the Bibliothèque de l'arsenal, Fonds Rondel.

53. Cf. Mme Marie-Jeanne Durry, pp. 98–101. On the other hand, Laforgue's aesthetic theory was markedly symbolist. See Daniel Grojnowski, "La poétique de Laforgue," *Critique*, No. 237 (février, 1967), 254–65.

54. Retté, *Le Symbolisme*, p. 200.

55. *Le Figaro*, le 12 décembre 1891.

56. Henry Fouquier, "L'Art Mystique," *Le Figaro*, le 15 décembre 1891.

57. "Chronique théâtrale," *Le Temps*, le 14 décembre 1891.

58. See *La Revue Indépendante*, XXI, No. 62 (décembre 1891), 419–22.

59. "Quinzaine Dramatique," *Revue d'Art Dramatique,* le 1ᵉʳ janvier 1892, p. 48.

60. *Mercure de France,* IV, No. 25 (janvier 1892), 83–84.

61. "Les Théâtres," *L'Ermitage,* III (le 31 janvier 1892), 53. I am grateful to Professor Robert G. Shedd for obtaining a copy of this review for me.

62. See Albert Sonnenfeld, "Hamlet the German and Jules Laforgue," *Yale French Studies,* No. 33 (1964), 92–100.

63. Cf. Jean-Louis Barrault, *Réflexions sur le théâtre* (Paris, 1949), p. 88; also see Barrault, *Nouvelles Réflexions sur le théâtre* (Paris, 1959), pp. 36; 205.

The Rest is Silence   BROOKS

1. *Revue Blanche,* XIX (juin, 1899). For some other comments on these performances, and for a survey of the Hamlet figure in this period, see René Taupin, "The Myth of Hamlet in France in Mallarmé's Generation," *Modern Language Quarterly,* XIV (December, 1953), 432–47.

2. Louis Ménard, "Le vrai Hamlet," *Revue Blanche,* XI (juillet, 1896), 20.

3. Stéphane Mallarmé, "Hamlet et Fortinbras," *Œuvres complètes* (Paris: Bibliothèque de la Pléiade, 1956), p. 1564. Originally published in the *Revue Blanche,* août 1896. Subsequent references to this article will give page number of the *Œuvres complètes* in parentheses in the text.

4. "Hamlet," *O.c.,* pp. 299–302, 301. This article was originally published in *La Revue Indépendante,* I, No. 1 —Nouvelle série, Iᵉʳ novembre, 1886. Subsequent references will give page numbers of the *O.c.* in parentheses in text.

5. "Le genre ou des modernes," *O.c.,* p. 312.

6. See Jacques Schérér, *Le "Livre" de Mallarmé* (Paris, 1957).

Since the present article was written, Haskell M. Block has published an interesting book on the question of Mallarmé's dramatic theories and his influence on the Symbolist theatre: *Mallarmé and the Symbolist Drama* (Detroit, 1963).

7. Villiers de l'Isle-Adam, *Oeuvres* (Paris: Club français du livre, 1957). Appendix.

8. *Ibid.*, p. 1015.

9. *Ibid.*, Appendix.

10. James Joyce, *Ulysses* (rev. ed.; New York, 1961), p. 187. Subsequent references will give page numbers in the text.

11. Jules Laforgue, *Moralités légendaires* (Paris: Mercure de France, 1954). p. 36. Subsequent references will give page numbers between parentheses in the text.

12. Villiers de l'Isle-Adam, *Oeuvres*, p. 1038.

13. Paul Valéry, "La crise de l'esprit," *Variété* (Paris, 1924), pp. 20–21.

14. Paul Claudel, "La Catastrophe d'Igitur," *Nouvelle Revue Française*, Iᵉʳ novembre, 1926.

15. Max Jacob, "L'Hamlétisme," *Art poétique* (Paris, 1922), p. 40.

Place of Laforgue
in Ezra Pound's Literary Criticism   DE NAGY

1. *Literary Essays* (London, 1954), p. 9.

2. *Le Problème du Style* (Paris, 1907), p. 157.

3. Donald Gallup, *A Bibliography of Ezra Pound*, London, 1963.

4. *Literary Essays*, p. 80.

5. Introduction to the *Literary Essays*, p. xi.

6. *Ibid.*, p. 306.

7. *Ta Hio: The Great Learning*, trans. Ezra Pound (London, 1936), p. 12.

8. *Letters*, ed. D. D. Paige (New York, 1950), p. 218.

9. *Literary Essays*, p. 282.

10. *Op. cit.*, Introduction, p. xiv.

11. *Letters*, p. 23.

12. *Literary Essays*, p. 32.

13. *Comparative Literature*, III (Winter, 1951), 48.

14. *Polite Essays* (London, 1937), p. 14.

15. *Literary Essays*, p. 281.

16. *Ibid.*, p. 282.

17. *Ibid.*, p. 283.

18. *Ibid.*, p. 282.

19. *Ibid.*, p. 33.

20. F. R. Leavis, *How to Teach Reading* (Cambridge, 1932), p. 12.

21. *Literary Essays*, p. 25.

22. *Ibid.*, p. 33.

23. François Ruchon, *Jules Laforgue, sa vie, son oeuvre* (Genève, 1924), p. 161.

24. "List of Books," *The Little Review*, IV (March 11, 1918), 57.

25. "Guitare" (p. 219), "Complainte du foetus du poète" (p. 94), "Complainte de la fin des journées" (p. 99), Laforgue, *Œuvres complètes*, I (Paris, 1922).

26. "Complainte de la fin des journées," *ibid.*, p. 99.

27. "Complainte des noces de Pierrot," *ibid.*, p. 142.

28. "Locutions des Pierrots," *ibid.*, p. 234.

29. *Literary Essays*, p. 25.

30. *Make It New* (London, 1934), p. 163.

31. "List of Books," *loc. cit.*, p. 57.

Laforgue and Samuel Beckett   OSTROVSKY

1. Guillaume Apollinaire's *Les Mamelles de Tirésias*; Jean Cocteau's *Parade* and *Les Mariés de la Tour Eiffel*; Eugène Ionesco's *La Cantatrice Chauve* and his remarks in "La Démystification par l'humour noir," L'Avant-Scène (10 Fevrier, 1959), pp. 5–6. See also, Roger Shattuck's discussion of Apollinaire and Cocteau in *The Banquet Years* (New York, 1948), pp. 120, 123, 142, 157–58, 188, and Anna Balakian's statements concerning Laforgue in her *Literary Origins of Surrealism* (New York, 1947), pp. 100, 110, 132.

2. Louis Ferdinand Céline's *Voyage au bout de la nuit*, his *Mort à crédit*, and Jean-Paul Sartre's *La Nausée*, stress such a view of existence. This reappears in the work of Beckett and will be explored in some detail in the course of this essay.

3. Ruby Cohn notes in her "Preliminary Observa-

tions," *Perspective*, II, No. 3 (1959), 119–31, that T. S. Eliot's influence on Beckett's early work manifests itself in an "insistence on conversational tone and irony, on thematic compression" (p. 119). These are precisely the qualities which characterize much of Laforgue's late work and which T. S. Eliot may have taken over from him. See also, Warren Ramsey's *Jules Laforgue and the Ironic Inheritance* (New York, 1953), pp. 192–204, on T. S. Eliot's indebtedness to Jules Laforgue, and G. M. Turnell's "The Poetry of Jules Laforgue," *Scrutiny* (Cambridge, England), II (1936), 128, 137.

4. Warren Ramsey notes that several of Laforgue's literary inventions anticipate those of James Joyce (pp. 139, 233). We know that James Joyce admired the *Moralités légendaires* of Laforgue, and while there is no direct mention of Laforgue in his work, it seems evident that many of his procedures coincide sufficiently with those of Laforgue to permit us at least to assume some link between the two writers. There seems little doubt that Beckett felt the impact of Joyce. This is the opinion of Kenneth Allsop in *The Angry Decade* (London, 1958), p. 38, and is shared by many other critics.

5. *Moralités légendaires* (Paris, 1946), pp. 19–72.

6. Paris, 1957.

7. The cupboard reappears in *Malone Dies* (New York, 1956), pp. 20, 90. In the second instance, it contains a poison by which life can be ended, just as in *Fin de partie*.

8. *The First Nine Books of the Danish History of Saxo Grammaticus*, trans. Oliver Elton (London, 1894), pp. 104–30, where the tale of Amleth, Prince of Jutland, is given, show that the names of Horwendill, Fengo, and Gerutha, which appear in Laforgue's tale, "Hamlet, ou les suites de la piété filiale," coincide with those of Saxo Grammaticus' story, as do other minor facts.

9. Mallarmé's figure of Igitur, especially as interpreted by Wallace Fowlie in his book *Mallarmé* (Chicago, 1953), has many of the characteristics which appear in Laforgue's Hamlet. Igitur, "a character who has felt in himself the existence of the absolute" (p. 113), suggests Hamlet, who

possesses "ce sixième sens, ce sens de l'infini" (*Moralités légendaires*, p. 36). Many other parallels can be found which would substantiate the fact that Hamlet incorporates some of Igitur's traits.

10. Richard Eastmann, "The Strategy of Samuel Beckett's 'Endgame,'" *Modern Drama*, II, 1 (1959), 39.

11. *Moralités légendaires*, p. 39.

12. Ray Walker, "Samuel Beckett's Double Bill, Love, Chess and Death," *Twentieth Century*, MCXIV, No. 982 (1958), 539.

13. *Œuvres complètes de Jules Laforgue*, ed. G. Jean-Aubry (Paris, 1951),—hereafter cited as O.c.—II, 167–72.

14. Jean-Jacques Mayoux, "The Theatre of Samuel Beckett," *Perspective*, II, No. 3 (1959), 154.

15. *Murphy* (New York, 1938), p. 65.

16. The *humour noir* of Laforgue appears in such poems as "Guitare," O.c., II, 201; "Excuse macabre," O.c., II, 203; "Complainte des blackboulés," O.c., I, 127; "Complainte du Pauvre corps humain," O.c., I, 147. It is also evident in some of the *Moralités légendaires*: "Hamlet . . ." (p. 52); "Salomé," (p. 172); "Lohengrin" (pp. 108, 110), "Les Deux Pigeons" (p. 272).

17. Examples of Laforgue's interior monologue can be found in much of his late work, but are clearest in "Hamlet . . ." (pp. 23–25, 34–36), and in such poems as "Solo de lune" (O.c., II, 167–72).

18. For example, in "L'Hiver qui vient" (O.c., II, 143–46).

19. Walker, p. 538.

20. *Watt* (New York, 1959), pp. 101–3.

21. O.c. I, 146–48; O.c., II, 200–1, etc.

22. Turnell, p. 132.

23. Mayoux, p. 154.

24. *Ibid*.

25. Samuel Beckett, *Proust* (New York, 1931), p. 47.

26. *Edition de la Connaissance*, II, 25.

27. *Murphy*, p. 111.

28. *Nouvelles et textes pour rien* (Paris, 1955), p. 74.

29. *Murphy*, p. 113.

30. *Stéphane Vassiliew* (Genève, 1946), p. 51.

31. Edith Kern, "Moran-Molloy, the Hero as Author," *Perspective*, II, No. 3 (1959), 190.

32. *O.c.*, I, 65.

33. *Edition de la Connaissance*, II, 111.

34. Pp. 50–51.

35. *Fin de partie*, pp. 33, 34; see also the expression of a similar feeling in *The Unnamable* (New York, 1958), p. 48.

36. "Hamlet . . . ," p. 46.

37. *The Unnamable*, p. 8.

38. "Stérilités," *O.c.*, I, 262.

39. *The Unnamable*, p. 23.

40. *Murphy*, p. 113.

41. *Malone Dies* (New York, 1956), p. 50.

42. *Ibid.*, p. 108.

43. *Ibid.*, p. 31.

44. *O.c.*, I, 259, 261, etc.

45. *The Unnamable*, p. 31.

46. "Notes on Eduard von Hartmann." Unpublished manuscript.

47. *The Unnamable*, p. 153.

48. *Nouvelles et textes . . .* , p. 181.

Phryne, or More Than One Right Word   RAMSEY

1. In *Sur les beaux lacs de l'idéal, des ronds dans l'eau*, Les Editions de Moghreb (Casablanca, 1941), p. 55.

2. This poem was first called "Le Véritable Amour," had an epigraph, crossed out in the MS, "Hamlet: the rest is silence," and the first six lines were in slightly different form:

Oh! qu'une, d'Elle-Même, un beau soir, sût venir!
Ne voyant que boire à Mes Lèvres, ou mourir!

Je m'enlève rien que d'y songer! Quel baptême
De gloire intrinsèque: attirer un "Je vous aime"!

L'attirer à travers la Société, de loin,
Comme l'aimant la Foudre. Un' deux! ni plus ni moins.
—f° 7 MS Bibliothèque Jacques Doucet A. III. 9

3. As published in *La Vogue*, December 6, 1886, the poems beginning, respectively, "Oh! qu'une, d'Elle-même, un beau soir, sût venir" and "O géraniums diaphanes, guerroyeurs sortilèges,"—published as Sections IX and X in what Dujardin and Fénéon, together with later editors, have called the *Derniers Vers*—was a single poem with the epigraph "Arrêtons-nous, amour, contemplons notre gloire—Petrarch."

4. Laforgue first wrote in a draft of the *Derniers Vers*:

> *Et qu'il vienne à travers les litières des*
> *hommes et des dieux*
> *—f° 143 MS Bibliothèque Jacques Dou-*
> *cet A. III. 9*

5. In the preserved MSS of this quatrain Laforgue wrote: "On durcira chacun chez soi." The next to last line went through several stages:

> *Et sûrement (oh! je m'y vois)*
> *Et sûrement (ah! je m'y vois)*
> *Et sûrement (que je m'y vois)*
> *Et bien sûr, comme je m'y vois!*
> *   et bien des fois*
> *   et plus d'une fois*

The last line passed through two preliminary stages:

> *On songera: Si j'avais su . . .*
> *On se dira: Si j'avais su!"*
> *—f° 122 Bibliothèque Jacques Doucet A. III. 9*

6. These two lines, like "Phrases, verroteries / Caillots de souvenirs" following, and key revisions in the longer lines "Adieu! les files d'ifs . . . tout s'en aille" further on, are added in black ink to MS otherwise written in red. The most characteristic and expressive forms represent the poet's second thoughts.

There is nothing resembling "Oh comme elle est amaigrie! / Que vais-je devenir! . . ." in this MS (f° 111 Bibliothèque Jacques Doucet A. III. 9).

7. Earlier version:

> *Caillots des souvenirs*
> *Phrases, verroteries*
> > (*this changed from:*
> > *Yeux en verroteries*)
>
> *Que vais-je devenir*
> *Oh! comme elle a maigri*
> > (*apparently changed from:*
> > *Oh! come elle est amaigrie . . .*)
> > —*f° 112 MS Bibliothèque Jacques Doucet*
> > *A. III. 9*

8. Earlier:

> *O Loi du Rythme sans appel!*
> > (*this from: O Loi du Rythme universel*)
>
> *Que le moindre Astre certifie*
> *Par son humble chorégraphie*
> *Aux infinis galas du ciel!*
> > (*added, to side: Mais nul Spectateur*
> > *éternel.*)
>
> *Ah! la Terre humanitaire*
> *N'en est pas moins terre-à-terre!*
> > —*"Petites misères d'août" f° 82 MS Biblio-*
> > *thèque Jacques Doucet A. III. 9*

Elsewhere:

> *O Loi du rythme universel*
> *Que le moindre astre certifie*
> *Par son humble chorégraphie*
> *Devant la barre sans appel*
> > —*"Grosses misères d'août," f° 83 Biblio-*
> > *thèque Jacques Doucet A. III. 9*

9. These lines are taken from the beginning of a poem called first "L'Idole," then "Notre campagne," then (as the Dujardin-Fénéon edition of the *Derniers Vers* does not note) "Notre petite campagne."

The four lines in f° 113 MS Bibliothèque Jacques Doucet A. III. 9 are vaguely punctuated, otherwise as given here.

10.

> *Je finirai par y prendre froid*
> —*"Grosses misères d'août," f° 83 MS*
> *Bibliothèque Jacques Doucet A. III. 9*

11.

Il dit: "Oh! t'enchanter la muqueuse du coeur!"
Elle dit: "Je n'ai plus rien à perdre à cett' heur',
La terre est en plein air, et ma vie est gâchée,
Ne songe qu'à la Nuit, je ne suis point fâché."
    —*f° 27 MS Bibliothèque Jacques Doucet A. III. 9*
    "Petites misères de Juillet"
"Oh! t'enchanter un peu la muqueuse du coeur!"
    ("Oh! t'enchanter là-bas la muqueuse du coeur!")
    (Il dit: "Oh! t'enchanter la muqueuse du coeur!")
Ah! Vas: "Je n'ai plus rien à perdre à cett' heur',
    (Elle dit: "Je n'ai plus rien à perdre à cett' heur',
"La terre est en plein air et ma vie est gâchée,
"Ne songe qu'à la Nuit, je ne suis point fâchée."
    —*f° 30 MS Bibliothèque Jacques Doucet A. III. 9*

Laforgue also approached the theme indirectly:

> *Rien ne les tient, rien ne les fâche,*
>   *(Rien ne les prend, rien ne les fâche)*
> *Elles veulent qu'on les trouve belles*
> *Qu'on le leur râle et leur rabâche,*
> *Et qu'on les use comme telles.*
>   —*"Esthétique," f° 106 Bibliothèque Jacques*
>   *Doucet A. III. 9*

12.

> *O soeurs! ensanglantez la terre, ce pressoir*
> —*f° 28 MS Bibliothèque Jacques Doucet A. III. 9*

13.

> *Soit, pas choisi*
> *Oui, pas choisi*
> *(preceded the present form)*
>   —*f° 83 MS Bibliothèque Jacques Doucet. A. III. 9*

14. These lines of verse, together with what immediately precedes and follows them, were added to the proofs of the *Moralités légendaires*. The complete handwritten passage is as follows:

> *Lohengrin déclame (fredonne) d'un accent exemplaire:*
>   [*the five lines of verse, each underlined*]
> *Mourir! Mourir! Oh, je ne veux pas mourir! Je veux voir toute la terre. Je veux savoir la vérité sur la jeune fille!*
>   *Il sanglote désespérément la face dans son oreiller. Elsa se penche vers sa tempe; et, sur sa tempe en fièvre, (elle souffle) avec une infernale sincérité, elle souffle:*
> —MS *Bibliothèque Jacques Doucet B. VII. 28*

Chronicle

1. Laforgue's military papers gave August 20 as his birthdate. The baptismal record of the Parish of San Francisco de Asís in Montevideo gives the earlier date, and Jules thought of August 16 as his birthday. See his letter to Kahn, August 6, 1885; and his notebook for 1884–85 (*Mercure de France*, Nov. 1, 1953, p. 439).

1860   August 16:[1] Jules Laforgue born in Montevideo, second son of Charles and Pauline Lacolley Laforgue. Charles, a native of Tarbes taken to Montevideo as a child, founded a small school and gave private lessons in French, Greek, and Latin. Pauline Lacolley, daughter of a French bootmaker and former légionnaire in the Uruguayan struggle for independence, was his pupil.

1866   Pauline Laforgue, her five children and the grandparents Laforgue sail for France. Charles, in banking business now, remains behind.

     Voyage from Montevideo to Bordeaux takes seventy-five days. Jules would remember his "black fits of spleen" and the sunsets.

1868   Charles appears in Tarbes to take his family, except two oldest boys, back to Montevideo.

1869–76   Jules and Emile boarding-pupils at Collège Impérial (Lycée, after 1870) in Tarbes. Jules finishes studies through *deuxième*. Awarded only one first prize, in Religious Education.

1875   Charles and Pauline Laforgue and their eight younger children return to France. An eleventh child born in Tarbes.

1876   October: the Laforgues move to Paris—66, rue des Moines, aux Batignolles, "a house with a garden."

     Jules enters Lycée Fontanes (Condorcet)

1877   April 6: death of Pauline Laforgue, following a miscarriage.

1878   After a year of Philosophy and three months of Rhetoric, and three unsuccessful attempts at the *baccalauréat* examinations, Jules' formal education ends.

1879   The Laforgues move to an apartment at 5, rue Berthollet, near the Val-de-Grace, convent turned military hospital.

Jules' first published poems, including a "Chanson de la Mort" and a son's versified dialogue with his father concerning need to choose an occupation, appear in little magazines in Tarbes and Toulouse. End of year, early 1880: plans for "a book of poems which I call philosophical. Unpretentiously, naïvely, I was a believer. Then a sudden tearing. Two years of solitude in the libraries, loveless, friendless, in fear of death . . . The book will be called *Le Sanglot de la Terre*."

1880   Early in year: meets Gustave Kahn at *Le Club des Hydropathes*.

Through Kahn he meets Charles Henry, future physiologist, and, through Henry, Mme. Mültzer, poetess.

September 20: during carnival following dedication of Lion de Belfort, conceives of *complainte* as literary form.

1880–81   Submits poems and stories to Paul Bourget for criticism.

Follows Taine's lectures on aesthetics and art history at Ecole des Beaux-Arts.

1881   Works as part-time assistant to Charles Ephrussi, art historian and editor.

September: family (except Emile, on military service) having returned to Tarbes, Jules lives in furnished room at 21, rue Monsieur-le-Prince.

November 18: death of Charles Laforgue, in Tarbes; Jules, on recommendations of Bourget and Ephrussi, appointed French reader to Empress Augusta of Germany, wife of Wilhelm I.

November 29: joins Court at Coblenz.

December 1: travels with Court to Berlin, where Empress usually resides from December till end of April.

Between May and mid-August, when Jules leaves for vacations in Paris and Tarbes, Empress's schedule calls for more or less regular stays in Baden-Baden, Berlin, Coblenz, Homburg, and Babelsberg Castle near Potsdam. But this itinerary is varied and in later years Jules travels considerably on his own, often to see exhibitions of paintings on which he sends *chroniques* to Ephrussi's *Gazette des Beaux-Arts*.

He rejoins Court in November, at Baden-Baden or Coblenz.

1881–82 Becomes close friend of Théophile Ysaÿe, pianist, brother of Eugène.

1882–83 Romantically involved with "R.," enigmatic personage attached to Court.

1882 February: acute dissatisfaction with early verse. November: sets to work seriously on *Complaintes*.

1883 August: has written forty of the fifty *Complaintes*. December: "shut away, cloistered in this castle at Coblenz" formulates an aesthetics centered on notion of a creative Unconscious which "bloweth where it listeth."

1884 March, writing to publisher Léon Vanier, with whom Charles Henry has arranged for publication of *Complaintes:* "The manuscript as you have received it is in final form. I want the printing to begin as soon as possible."

July, Isle of La Mainau, Lake Constance: writes most of *L'Imitation de Notre-Dame la Lune*.

July–October, at Kassel and in Paris: writes more *complaintes*, including "Complainte des Pianos" and "Grande complainte de la ville de Paris."

1885 July 25: *Les Complaintes de Jules Laforgue*. September 1: Gustave Kahn, with whom Laforgue has spent two days at Strasbourg in mid-June, visits Berlin.

December 5: *La Bibliographie de la France* announces publication of *L'Imitation de Notre-Dame la Lune* (book bears date of 1886).

1886 January: begins English lessons with Leah Lee.

March: Téodor de Wyzewa and Edouard Dujardin, launching the new *Revue Indépendante*, look up Laforgue in Berlin.

June–August: his translations from "l'étonnant poète américain Walt Whitman" appear in *La Vogue*, periodical edited by Léo d'Orfer and Gustave Kahn.

June–November: five of the tales to be called *Moralités légendaires* appear in *La Vogue*.

July: "Le Concile féerique" published in *La Vogue* and as separate pamphlet.

August–December: poems which would be called *Derniers Vers* appear in *La Vogue*.

September 8: writes to sister Marie that he and Leah are engaged.

September 9: leaves Berlin, giving up readership.

December 31: marriage at Saint Barnabas Church, Addison Road, Kensington.

1887 At 8, rue de Commaille in Paris, Jules' "three-months' cold" continuing, Laforgues live on proceeds of his articles, including contributions to an imaginary Russian periodical conceived by Téodor de Wyzewa.

July: Jules corrects proof for *Moralités légendaires*. Publisher declines his *Berlin, la cour et la ville* unless he will amplify sections on court life, shorten those dealing with the town, and let his name and former functions appear on cover of book.

August 10: writes trying to arrange two weeks' stay in Versailles, where he would be able to breathe "a purer air."

August 20: death at 8, rue de Commaille.

November: *Moralités légendaires*.

December 5: Leah Laforgue, in Paris on her way from England to the House for Consumption at

Menton, writes to Téodor de Wyzewa: "I . . . have before I go a kindness to beg you relative to my husband's papers."

1888   June 11: death of Leah Laforgue at St. Peter's Home, Kilburn.

1890   *Les Derniers Vers de Jules Laforgue,* edited by Dujardin and Felix Fénéon.

1894   *Poésies complètes,* with preface by Dujardin.

1922   *Berlin, la Cour et la Ville.*

Bibliography

Les Complaintes, L'Imitation de Notre-Dame la Lune, Moralités légendaires, Derniers Vers, Berlin, la cour et la ville and other works of Jules Laforgue are noted in the preceding chronicle. To these should be added:

Stéphane Vassiliew, edited with introduction by François Ruchon. Geneva, 1946.

"Carnet 1884–85," ed. Isabelle de Wyzewa, *Mercure de France*, CCCXIX (octobre–novembre 1953), 202–15, 426–43.

Lettres à un ami (1880–1886). With introduction and notes by G. Jean-Aubry. Mercure de France, 1941.

"Cinq poèmes inconnus de Jules Laforgue," *Revue des sciences humaines*, Sér. 2, Nos. 65–72 (octobre–décembre 1953), 365–77.

Feuilles, textes publiés par Daragniès pour "Nous Quatre" (G. Jean-Aubry, Jean Gabriel Daragniès, Jules Laloux, Lucien Jaïs). Montmartre, 1941. Reprinted in *Mercure de France*, CCCL (Avril 1964), 616–23.

Editions:

Œuvres complètes, ed. G. Jean-Aubry, 6 vols. Mercure de France, 1922–30. I and II, *Poésies*. III, *Moralités légendaires*. IV and V, *Lettres*. VI, *En Allemagne: Berlin, la cour et la ville; Une Vengeance à Berlin; Agenda de 1883*.

Œuvres complètes, 3 vols. Mercure de France, 1901–3. I, *Moralités légendaires*. II, *Poésies*. III, *Mélanges posthumes*.

Editions de la Connaissance, 3 vols., 1920–21. I, *Chroniques Parisiennes, Ennuis non rimés*, ed. André Malraux.

II, *Dragées, Charles Baudelaire, Tristan Corbière,* ed. André Malraux. III, *Exil, Poésie, Spleen,* ed. René-Louis Doyon.

Les Complaintes, L'Imitation de Notre-Dame la Lune, Derniers Vers. Edited with with introduction by Claude Pichois, 1959.

Derniers Vers. Edited with introduction and notes by Michael Collie and J. M. L'Heureux. Toronto, 1965.

Poésie complète, 2 vols. Edited by Sergio Cigada with introduction by Sergio Solmi. Edizioni dell' Ateneo, Rome, 1966.

Concerning Laforgue (Selective)

Arkell, David. "Leah Laforgue." *Times Literary Supplement,* No. 3302 (June 10, 1965), 480.

Austin, L. J. *Paul Bourget, sa vie et son oeuvre jusqu'en 1889.* Geneva: Droz, 1940.

Bachelard, Gaston. *L'Eau et les rêves: Essai sur l'imagination de la Matière.* Corti, 1942.

———. *La Terre et les rêveries de la volonté.* Corti, 1948.

Bailey, Helen Phelps. *Hamlet in France, from Voltaire to Laforgue (with an Epilogue).* Geneva: Droz, 1964.

Beaunier, André. *La Poésie nouvelle.* Mercure de France, 1902, pp. 73–79.

Benamou, Michel. "Laforgue and Wallace Stevens." *Romanic Review,* L (April 1959), 107–17.

Blin, Georges. "A la Recherche de l'infini: Laforgue et Baudelaire," *Revue Hebdomadaire,* XLVII (5 novembre 1938), 84–93.

Bolgar, R. R. "The Present State of Laforgue Studies," *French Studies,* IV, July 1950.

Brunfaut, Marie. *Jules Laforgue, les Ysaÿe et leur temps.* Bruxelles, 1961.

Carrière, J. M. "Jules Laforgue and Leopardi," *Romanic Review,* XXXIV (February 1943), 50–53.

Chamberlain, Houston S. *Lebenswege meines Denkens.* Munich, 1919, pp. 332–4.

Champigny, Robert. "Situation of Jules Laforgue," *Yale French Studies,* No. 9 (1952), 63–73.

Clouard, Henri. "La Poésie de Jules Laforgue," *Le Divan,* XV (mai 1923), 261–9.

Collie, Michael. *Laforgue.* ("Writers and Critics Series.") Edinburgh and London, 1963.

Cuisinier, Jeanne. *Jules Laforgue.* Paris, 1925.

Doyon, René-Louis. "La Canne de Jules Laforgue et la statue de Bobillot," *Les Livrets du Mandarin,* Sér. 4, No. 2, novembre 1939.

Dufour, Médéric. *Une Philosophie de l'Impressionisme. Etude sur l'esthétique de Jules Laforgue,* 1904.

Dujardin, Edouard. *Les Premiers Poètes du vers libre.* Mercure de France, 1922.

Durry, Marie-Jeanne, *Jules Laforgue.* ("Poètes d'aujourd'-hui.") Seghers, 1952.

Eliot, T. S. "The Metaphysical Poets," *Homage to John Dryden,* 1924.

———. Introduction, *Selected Poems of Ezra Pound,* 1928.

———. "Donne in Our Time," *A Garland for John Donne,* 1931.

———. "On a Recent Piece of Criticism," *Purpose,* April–June 1938.

———. "Propos," *Une Semaine dans le monde,* 1 mai, 1948.

———. "Talk on Dante," *The Adelphi,* XXVII, No. 2 (1951), 106–14.

Fargue, Léon-Paul. "Jules Laforgue," *Revue de Paris.* (avril 1935), pp. 783–90.

Fowlie, Wallace. "Jules Laforgue," *Poetry,* LXXVIII (July 1951), 216–22.

Golffing, Francis C. "Jules Laforgue," *Quarterly Review of Literature,* III (Summer 1946), 55–67.

Gourmont, Remy de. *Le Livre des masques,* 1896, pp. 203–9.

———. *Promenades littéraires,* 4° série (1910), 105–10.

Greene, E. J. H. *T. S. Eliot et la France.* Boivin-Didier, 1951.

Grojnowski, Daniel. "La Poétique de Laforgue," *Critique,* No. 237 (février, 1967), 254–65.

Guichard, Léon. *Jules Laforgue et ses poésies.* Presses Universitaires de France, 1950.

Hays, H. R. "Laforgue and Wallace Stevens," *Romanic Review*, XXV (1934), 242–48.

Henriot, Emile. "Jules Laforgue ou le démon de la nouveauté," *Poetes français de Lamartine à Valéry*. Lyon: Landarchet, 1946.

Jones, P. Mansell. *The Assault on French Literature and Other Essays*. Manchester, 1963.

Kahn, Gustave. *Symbolistes et Décadents*. Vanier, 1902, pp. 181–99.

———. "Jules Laforgue," Mercure de France, CLX (décembre 1922), 289–313.

Kenner, Hugh. *The Invisible Poet: T. S. Eliot*. New York, 1959.

Mauclair, Camille. *Essai sur Jules Laforgue*. Mercure de France, 1896. With introduction by Maurice Maeterlinck.

———. "Le Cinquantenaire de Jules Laforgue," *Revue de Paris*, (15 juillet, 1937), 341–51.

Meesemaeker, G. *Jules Laforgue*. Hanoï-Haïphong, 1922.

Miomandre, Francis de. "Jules Laforgue," *Mercure de France*, XLV (1903), 289–314.

———. "Notes et impressions sur Jules Laforgue," *Revue de Paris* (août 1937), 666–71.

Newman-Gordon, Pauline. *Corbière, Laforgue, Apollinaire*. Paris: Debresse, 1963.

Pérès, Jean. "Anticipations des principes de la psychanalyse dans l'oeuvre d'un poète français," *Journal de psychologie normale et pathologique*, 19e année (1922), 921–7.

Pound, Ezra. "Irony, Laforgue and Some Satire," *Poetry*, XI (November 1917), 93–8. Reprinted in *Literary Essays of Ezra Pound*, London, 1960.

———. "A Study of French Modern Poets," *Little Review*, February, 1918. Reprinted with minor changes in *Instigations*, 1920, and *Make it New*, 1935, pp. 159–247.

Quennell, Peter. *Baudelaire and the Symbolists*, London, 1929. Second revised edition, 1954.

Ramsey, Warren. *Jules Laforgue and the Ironic Inheritance*. New York, 1953.

Régnier, Henri de. *Faces et profils; souvenirs sur Villiers de l'Isle-Adam, Jules Laforgue, Stéphane Mallarmé*, 1931. The same essay, "Jules Laforgue," in *Nos Rencontres*, 1931.

Rivière, Jacques. *Correspondance, J. Rivière et Alain-Fournier, 1905–1914*, 1926–8.

——. "Alain-Fournier," *Nouvelle Revue Française*, XIX (décembre 1922), 643–68. Reprinted as introduction to *Miracles*, 1924.

Ruchon, François. *Jules Laforgue, sa vie, son oeuvre*. Geneva, 1924.

Smith, William Jay. Introductory essays in his *Selected Writings of Jules Laforgue*, 1956.

Sonnenfeld, Albert. "Hamlet the German and Jules Laforgue," *Yale French Studies*, No. 33 (1964), 92–100.

Souza, Robert de. "Un Cinquantenaire: Jules Laforgue, l'homme et l'oeuvre," *Mercure de France*, CCLXXIX (1 novembre 1937), 453–87.

Symons, Arthur. "The Decadent Movement in Literature," *Harper's New Monthly Magazine*, LXXXVII (November 1893), 858–67.

——. *The Symbolist Movement in Literature*. Heinemann, London, 1899.

Taupin, René. *L'Influence du symbolisme français sur la poésie américaine (de 1910–1920)*, 1929.

Terry, Patricia. Introduction to *Poems of Jules Laforgue*. Translated by Patricia Terry, 1958. Foreword by Henri Peyre.

Turnell, Martin. "The Poetry of Jules Laforgue," *Scrutiny*, V (September 1936), 128–49.

——. "Jules Laforgue," *Cornhill Magazine*, No. 973 (Winter 1947–8), 74–90.

Unger, Leonard. *The Man in the Name: Essays on the Experience of Poetry*. Minneapolis, 1956.

Vial, Fernand. "L'inconscient métaphysique et ses premières expressions littéraires en France: Jules Laforgue." *Stil- und Formprobleme* V, 358–66.

Wyzewa, Téodor de. *Nos Maîtres, études et portraits littéraires*, Perrin, 1895.

Index

Adams, Léonie, 163
Appollinaire, Guillaume, 46, 81, 110, 130, 154
Augusta, the Empress, xvii, 29, 179

Balzac, Honoré de, 71
Banville, Théodore de: and literary theatre, 77, 86; and clown figure, 81; and Symbolists, 86; verse play, 88
Barrault, Jean-Louis: in adaptation of "Hamlet," 91
Baudelaire, Charles: Laforgue's Notes on, xxi, xxii, 31, 58; irony and *le surnaturel*, xxi, 33, 34; and *l'angoisse métaphysique*, xxi–xxii, 31–32, 58; on *le mal* as a force, xxii, 34, 38; as *poète absolu*, 26, 27; and Rimbaud, 27; theme of Ennui, 29; and Poe, 32, 33, 41; on nature of Beauty, 34, 99; and ideal of modernity, 38; influence compared to Laforgue's, 41, 117; contrasted with Heine, 58. *See also* Eliot; Mallarmé; Poe
—"Correspondances," 35; "Le Cygne," xxi; "Duellum," 36; *Les Fleurs du Mal*, 26–28, 39, 66–67; "L'Invitation au voyage," 36; "Les Phares," 35; "Un Voyage à Cythère," 37–38
Beckett, Samuel: and Laforgue's darker humor, xxvii, 130, 131; "Hamlet" and *Fin de partie*, 131–45; and "le Saint-Sépulcre maternel," 141, 143, 144, 145; *L'Innommable*, 142–43, 144–45
Bergson, Henri, 50
Berlin, la cour et la ville, xvii–xix, 181, 182
Bogan, Louis, 163
Bourget, Paul: on poetry, xxiii; as critic of Laforgue, xxiv, 76–77, 179; recommends Laforgue, 179; mentioned, xix
Breton, André: on Naturalism, 47
Buddhism: stages of Laforgue's, xx, xxiii, xxv, 67; and Idealism, xxiii
Burke, Kenneth: and "tangent ending" of poem, 6, 14, 163

Cendrars, Blaise, 46
Claudel, Paul, 44, 109
Cocteau, Jean, 46, 130
Commedia dell'arte, xv, 79, 157
Les Complaintes: and the *complainte populaire*, xv; recitals at *Club des Hydropathes*, 77; genesis, Laforgue's volume, 179–80. For *complainte* form and individual poems, *see* Laforgue
Le Concile féerique: attitudes expressed in, 83, 84, 153; composite form of, 83, 152; ballet-like, 85, 157; akin to *proverbe* and dramatic ode, 86; performance and critical reaction, 89–91; taut organization of, 154
"Conversation Galante"; and *Le*

Concile féerique, 153; mentioned, 69

Corbière, Tristan: and Laforgue, xxii, 47, 71, 74; and Eliot, 15; and Pound, 15, 116, 123

Crane, Hart: and translations of Laforgue, 6–7; mentioned, xiv, xix, 163

Cummings, E. E., 6, 71, 163

Damon, S. Foster, 6, 163

"Decadents," the: Laforgue and, xxiv, 110; their style, 55–56; and theatre, 95; and Hamlet-figure, 96, 101; and purity, 100; symbolizing faculty, 104. *See also* Huysmans; Villiers

Delacroix, Eugène, 93

Derniers Vers: free verse of, xviii, xxv, xxix, 49, 75, 147–48, 160–61; self-affirmation in, 35–36; womankind in, 36; force of negation in, 36

Desnos, Robert, 46

Donne, John, 41–42

Dujardin, Edouard, xix, 181, 182

Eliot, T. S.: influence as understood by Eliot and Gourmont, xiii, xxix; discovery of a poetic personage, xxix, 14; discovery of a form in Laforgue, xxix, 14, 42; anticipations of "Prufrock" in *Harvard Advocate* poems, 5, 112; Laforguian elements in "Prufrock," 14; "form . . . drawn from the study of Laforgue together with the later Elizabethans," 41; linked with "English metaphysicals" and Corbière, 41; "pattern . . . given by what goes on within the mind," 41; seemed to speak more directly than Baudelaire, 41; Laforgue "inventor of an attitude," 42; Eliot among Symbolists, 67; development, 68–69; other Laforguian poems, 111; some consequences for Anglo-

American poetry, 114; thought and feeling unified, 128. *See also* Corbière; "Decadents"; Pound

—"Conversation Galante," 69, 153; "La Figlia che Piange," 69; Four Quartets, 74, 130; "Fragment of an Agon," 15; "The Hippopotamus," 15; "Portrait of a Lady," 150; "Prufrock," xxix, 9, 14, 42, 111, 112; "The Use of Poetry and the Use of Criticism," 48; *The Waste Land*, 15, 42–43

Ephrussi, Charles, xix, xxiii, 179, 180

Fénéon, Felix, 182

Flaubert, Gustave: satire of, xxvi, 61, 122, 123; Pound on, 116, 118, 122, 123; as "true Penelope," 160

Les Fleurs du Mal: as model and force, 26, 39; and Symbolists, 27, 39, 66–67; language in, 33–34

Des Fleurs de bonne volonté: attitudes in, 34, 35; drawn on for *Le Concile féerique*, 83, 85; and *Derniers Vers*, 147–52

Flint, F. S., 39

Ford, Ford Madox, 118, 121

Fouquier, Henri, 90

Fournier, Alain-, 44

Free Verse: importance of Laforgue's, xviii, 58, 120–21; Impressionist responsiveness of, xxviii, 147, 160–61; Pound on, 121

Gautier, Théophile: and Imagist aims, 116–17; mentioned, 40, 45, 49

Gide, André: Laforguian *Paludes*, 48; mentioned, 40, 44

Giraudoux, Jean, xxvi

Goethe: echoed in "Hamlet," 107; mentioned, 46, 48, 77

Gourmont, Remy de: liberating

force of work, xiii; on Laforgue, xiv, xv; on new direction within a literature, 112;
mentioned, 88
Granval, Charles, 91

"Hamlet, ou les suites de la
piété filiale": and Mallarmé's
"Ouverture ancienne," 72–
73; growth of dramatic power
in, 91; stage adaptations, 91;
as expression of Decadent
mind and mood; 101–10; and
Flaubert's "Légende de St.-
Julien," 103; parallels with
Beckett's Fin de partie, 131–
45
Hartmann, Eduard von, Philosophy of the Unconscious,
xxiii, 53. See also Unconscious, the
Heine, Heinrich: and irony, xxv;
contrasted with Baudelaire,
58; and "Logopoeia," 124
Henry, Charles, xx, 79, 82, 147,
179, 180
Hugo, Victor, 45, 46, 50, 71
Hulme, T. E., 68
Huneker, James Gibbons, 60
Huret, Jules: Enquête sur l'évolution littéraire, 52, 54, 163–64
Huysmans, Joris-Karl: A Rebours, xxiii–xxiv, 52; on Laforgue, 60; Pierrot sceptique,
79

Imagism: and Gautier's Emaux
et Camées, 116–17; and Symbolism, 117; and "phano-
poeia," 124; mentioned, xxiv.
See also Pound
L'Imitation de Notre-Dame la
Lune: imagery in, 143, 144
Irony: Laforgue's use of, xxiv–
xxv, 34, 45; controlling metaphors, 4; on romantic irony,
45; and a line of poets, 45;
origins, characteristics, 58,
121–22. See also Eliot; Heine;
Musset
Irving, Henry, 78

Jacob, Max: and Imagist, xxiv;
and Laforgue, 46; and Hamlet figure, 109; and clown-
figure, 110
Jarry, Alfred, 71, 93, 110
Joyce, James: and use of myths,
xxvi, 63; on Mallarmé and
Hamlet, xxvii, 99–100; and
Symbolism, 67; mentioned,
68, 136

Kahn, Gustave: meets Laforgue,
xxiii, 55, 77, 179; letters to,
67, 72; and La Vogue, 88,
181; visits Berlin, 180
Keats, John, 44, 63

Labat, Marie (née Laforgue),
xvii, xix, 163, 181
Laforgue, Charles, xxii, 178,
179
Laforgue, Emile, xxiii, 76–77,
178, 179
Laforgue, Jules: and Eliot, xiii,
xix, 5, 14, 41, 42, 43, 111,
114, 116, 117, 118, 119–20,
122, 123, 124–26, 127–28; a
poetry of understatement,
xiii–xiv, 82; Parnassian beginnings, xiv, xxii, 49; and
Crane, xiv, xxix, 6–7, 163;
Romantic survivals, xv, xix,
xxvii, 45, 86; a new form, the
literary complainte, xv, xxvii,
77–78, 180; literary criticism,
xxi, xxii, 31, 58; Baudelairean
echoes, xxi, 30–31, 36, 37; in
Paris, xxii, 55, 76–78, 178–
79; and Mallarmé, xxiv,
xxv, 28, 66–75; and Symbolism, xxiv–xxx, 28, 58, 67–68,
146–47; poetics of the Complaintes, L'Imitation de Notre-
Dame la Lune and Moralités
légendaires, xxiv–xxvi, 7, 8–9,
11–12, 14, 33, 34, 60–65, 77,
80–81, 125–27; Laforgue and
Heine, xxv, 58; Des Fleurs de
bonne volonté and Derniers
Vers, vers libéré and vers
libre, a poetics of alternatives,
xxx, 49, 147–48, 160–61; and

Pound, 5, 15, 40, 111, 114, 116, 117, 118, 119–20, 122–28; and Verlaine, 28; and Rimbaud, 28; early verse and projects, 30–31, 32, 45, 48, 49, 70–71, 75, 179; theatre, 76–92, 156–57; art criticism, 159, 161, 180; early years in Montevideo and Tarbes, 178; first four years in Germany, 179–81; last year in Germany and return to Paris, 179–82. *See also* entries for individual works; and Baudelaire; and Bourget; Gourmont; Huysmans; Taine; Valery; Irony; Symbolism; Unconscious, the —"Air de biniou," 34; "Arabesques de malheur," 149; "Autre Complainte de Lord Pierrot," 34; "Autre Complainte de l'orgue de Barbarie," 58; *Berlin, la cour et la ville*, xvii, xviii, xix, 181, 182; *Chroniques Parisiennes*, xviii; "La Cigarette," 45; "Climat, faune et flore de la Lune," 144; *Les Complaintes*, xiv, xv, 41, 81, 152, 160, 175, 180; "Complainte de l'automne monotone," 57; ". . . des noces de Pierrot," 127; ". . . des Nostalgies préhistoriques," 6–7; ". . . des Pianos qu'on entend dans les quartiers aisés," 10, 30, 180; ". . . du Roi de Thulé," 155; *Le Concile féerique*, 82–91, 153, 154, 181; *Derniers Vers*, xxii, xxv, xxix, 35–37, 147–48, 149, 150, 151, 152, 154, 181, 182; "Dimanches" (Bref, j'allais me donner . . . , 35; "Dimanches" (C'est l'automne), 150; "Dimanches" (Oh! ce piano . . .), 70; "Figurez-vous un peu," 147; *Des Fleurs de bonne volonté*, 34, 38, 70, 83, 85, 147, 149, 152; "Grande Complainte de la ville de Paris," 180; "Hamlet, ou les suites de la piété

familiale," xxvi, xxvii, 62, 72–73, 91, 101–10, 131–35, 142; "L'Hiver qui vient," 35, 74, 75; *L'Imitation de Notre-Dame la Lune*, 46, 119, 143, 144, 181; "Légende," 150–52; "Locutions des Pierrots," 7; "Lohengrin, fils de Parsifal," 62, 154, 155; "Le Miracle des roses," 63, 64; *Moralités légendaires*, xxv, xxvi, xxvii, xxviii, xxix, 5, 33, 60–65, 72–73, 91, 101–10, 131–45, 157–58, 181; "Noire bise . . . ," 37; "Notre Petite Campagne," 150; "Oh! qu'une, d'Elle-même . . . ," 147–48; "Pan et la Syrinx," xxvi, 73, 157–58; "Persée et Andromède," 60–61, 61–62, 73, 108; "Pétition," 36; "Petites Misères de juillet," 152; *Pierrot fumiste*, 79–81, 82, 156–67; "La Première Nuit," 30; "Salomé," xxv, xxix, 61, 73, 142; *Le Sanglot de la terre*, 30, 45, 48, 75, 179; "Simple Agonie," 36; "Solo de lune," 36, 149; *Stéphane Vassiliew*, xxviii

Laforgue, Leah (née Lee), xvi, xvii, xx, 16–25, 181, 182

Laforgue, Pauline Lacolley, 178

Lautréamont, Comte de (Isidore Ducasse), 71

Leclerq, Julien, 90–91

Leconte de Lisle, 48, 49, 50, 54

Lodge, George Cabot, 4

"Lohengrin, fils de Parsifal": Laforguian motif in, 62, 154–55; imagery in, 154–55

Maeterlinck, Maurice, 88, 89, 90

Mallarmé, Stéphane: and Laforgue's poetry, xiv, xxiv, 28, 72; Laforgue on, xiv, 67; on *Moralites légendaires*, xxv, 72; memorializes chance, 27; Baudelairean period, 27, 31; as Symbolist, 27, 39; his *Grand Oeuvre*, 32, 70; and

Joyce, 40–41, 99; and Poe, 41; on art of poetry, 48; Parnassian textures, 49; idea of a theatre, 81, 87; looks to theatre, 86, 95; and Symbolist drama, 87; and *Hamlet*, 93; on *Hamlet*, 94–95, 96–98, 100–101, 102, 104, 107; *Le Livre*, 95. *See also* Baudelaire; "Decadents," the; Gautier; Symbolism
—"L'Après-midi d'un faune," 52, 86; *Un Coup de Dés*, 27, 69, 71, 73, 74; "Hérodiade" Ouverture ancienne), 72–73, "Hérodiade" (Scène), 95; "Igitur," xxvii, 70, 95, 101, 109; "Notes sur le théatre," 87; poems in prose, 45, 69; "Prose pour des Esseintes," 72, 100; sonnets, 72, 74, 96, 97

Margueritte, Paul, 81
Mauclair, Camille: on *Le Concile féerique*, 86
Mendès, Catulle, 86, 88
"The Metaphysical Poets": Eliot links Laforgue with, 42, 128
"Le Miracle des roses": symbols in, xxvi, 63–65
Moody, William Vaughn, 4
Moralités lègendaires: myths in, xxv, xxvi, 61–63, 157–58; realistic tales excluded from, xxvi; language in, 60–61
Moréas, Jean, 44, 52
Moreau, Gustave, 73
Mültzer, Mme, 179
Musset, Alfred de: and irony, xxv, xxvii, 45, 46; and poets' theatre, xxvii, 77, 81, 86; mentioned, 58

Naturalism, 47, 52
Nerval, Gérarde de: and "Complainte du Roi de Thulé," 155; mentioned, 45, 50, 51
Nouveau théatre: and Laforgue, xxvi–xxvii, xxix, 131–45

Orfer, Léo d', 181

"Pan et la Syrinx": as explanation of art, 73, 158; and "L'Après-midi d'un faune," 73; mentioned, xxvi
Parnasse Contemporain, Third, xxii, 54
Péret, Benjamin, 46
"Persée et Andromède": modernity of characters, 61–62; indifference of nature, 73; style in keeping with subject, 108
Pierrot fumiste: likened to *Pierrot sceptique*, 79; begins with badinage, ends with scenario, 80; ironic-comic mask that of Lord Pierrot, 80; a persistent motif, 156–57
Poe, Edgar Allan: "Eureka," 31, 71; on controlled composition, 32, 159–60; love and death in, 41; in France, 41
"Portrait of a Lady": and draft of "Légende," 150
Pound, Ezra: introduced to Laforgue by Eliot, 5; paraphrase from "Salomé," 5; "logopoeia," descriptive of Laforgue's poetry, 8, 124–26, 128, 129; "never deeply influenced by Laforgue," 15; study of Nōh plays and development of Symbolist theatre, 95; Laforguian procedures, 111; an instrumental criticism applied to Laforgue, 114; Laforgue in "ideogram of good writing," 116, 118; Laforgue "marks next phase after Gautier," 117; from compound to complex verse, 119–20; emphasis on satire in Laforgue, 122, 123, 128; "logopoeia" a principle leading beyond Imagism, 127–28, 129; translations of "Pierrots (Scène courte mais typique)," 127–28
"Prufrock": Laforguian characteristics of, 9, 14, 42, 111–12

"R.," xvii, 180
Régnier, Henri de, 44, 49, 68

Renan, Ernest: and Hellenic ideal, 159
Retté, Adolphe, 88–89
Richards, I. A., 45
Rimbaud, Arthur: compared with Laforgue, xxviii, 28; as *voyant*, 27, 32; as Symbolist, 27, 39, 67; "only isomer of Baudelaire," 28, 36; before the Louvre, 36; impossible to imitate, 42; "Le Coeur supplicié," 49; *Les Illuminations*, 52; Pound on, 116, 117
Rivière, Jacques, 44
Rollinat, Maurice, 77, 78
Ronsard, Pierre de, 34
Rousseau, Henri, 109–10

"Salomé": as parody of "Hérodias," xxv, 61; and "Hérodiade," 73; and the Unconscious, 73; aquarium imagery in, 141
Samain, Albert, 44, 68
Le Sanglot de la terre: and Baudelaire, 30–31; as poetry of ideas, 48–49, 179; and Parnassians, 49; mentioned, 75
Sarcey, Francisque, 89, 90
Savonarola: projected drama on, 75
Schlegel, Friedrich, 45
Schopenhauer, Arthur: influence c. 1880, xxii, 50, 53
Shakespeare: and poets' theatre, 77; and *Hamlet* in '80's and '90's, 93–94; and "Hamlet," 101–4, 106; mentioned, 66
Spencer, Herbert: on ultimate causes, xxiii, 53; on society as organism, 53
Stendhal, 58, 118, 160
Stéphane Vassiliew: and a stage of Laforgue's prose, xxviii
Stevens, Wallace, 34
Stickney, Trumbull, 4
Supervielle, Jules, xxviii, 50
Surrealists, the, 46, 47, 130
Symbolism: and dynamics of language, xxiv; extension of term, xxiv, 68; associated with Greek classicism, 4; impact of, 39; manifesto, 52; associated with classicism, 67; and theatre, 86–89, 95; and unique poetic word, 146. *See also* Mallarmé; Wagner
Symons, Arthur, 42

Taihade, Laurent, 15, 57
Taine, Hippolyte: reaction to his aesthetic criteria, xx, 159–60; and determinism, xx, xxi, 159; and Hellenic ideal, 159; Laforgue follows Beaux-Arts lectures, 179
Tate, Allen, 163

Unconscious, the: as metaphysical principle, xxi, xxv, 50, 53, 67, 159, 160, 180; in creative process, 50, 141, 159, 160, 180

Valéry, Paul: and Poe, 41; and Rilke, 41; as Symbolist, 67, and Descartes, 70; and Hamlet-figure, 104, 109; "Mémoires d'un poème" and Laforgue's poetics, 161
Verlaine, Paul: compared with Laforgue, 28; on Baudelaire, 31; as Symbolist, 67
Vers libre. *See* Free Verse
Vielé-Griffin, 44, 68
Vigny, Alfred de, 50
Villiers de l'Isle Adam: his conception of *Hamlet* compared with Laforgue's, xxvii, 109; and literary theatre, 77; and realities of theatre, 95–96; *Hamlet* becomes idealist-materialist debate, 96; *Axël*, 97, 99, 101, 102, 103, 106, 107–8, 109; mentioned, 71
Villon, François, 27, 46, 116, 123
Vogüé, Melchior de, 54
Voltaire, xxv, 46, 72

Wagner, Richard: on music and poetry, 53–54; and literary theatre, 77; mentioned, 74

The Waste Land: and "Prufrock," 15; reviewed in 1923, 42–43

Whitman, Walt: Laforgue's translations from, xviii, 181

Williams, William Carlos, 71

Winter, Yvor, 163

Woolf, Virginia, 136

Wyzewa, Téodor de, 181–82

Yeats, William Butler, 40, 43, 68, 95, 98

Ysaÿe, Théophile, 180

Zola, Émile, 47